RAMBLING -
THE BEGINNER'S BIBLE

A Handbook For Country Walking

By John Bainbridge
Author of "The Compleat Trespasser"

Fellside Books

First Published by Fellside Books in paperback in 2014

EBook Kindle and Ereader edition 2013

Copyright © John Bainbridge 2013/14

advice given is intended to be definitive or official. Please note that you undertake any activities detailed herein at your own risk.

About The Author

John Bainbridge is a freelance journalist, the author of some thirty topographical books and many articles on the outdoors in magazines and newspapers. He has been a rambler and hillwalker for over fifty years, and was recently commended by the Ramblers Association for his many years of voluntary work in the rambling movement. John spent nine years as chief executive of the Dartmoor Preservation Association, fending off threats to the Dartmoor National Park. He is an outspoken advocate of ramblers' rights and the freedom to roam.

Visit John's Blog and Website:

Blog: www.stravaigerjohn.wordpress.com

Websites: www.johnbainbridgewriter.com and www.johnbainbridgejournalist.com

Introduction

Walking in the countryside is our most popular recreation and rambling is certainly the best way to get to know the quieter places of the British Isles. Unlike a lot of outdoor activities, rambling can be enjoyed by all kinds of people, young and old, those who are fighting fit and not quite so fit. You can go as far and do as much or as little as you choose. Rambling is all about taking time out from our very rushed modern world. An opportunity to walk away from the stress and travails of modern life.

Exploring Britain on foot has the added advantage that it brings people back to the land, opening up a whole world of other interests, whether it be history and archaeology, watching wildlife, or following in the steps of our ancestors on ancient tracks. The Victorian country writer Richard Jefferies said that *"Those only know a country who are acquainted with its footpaths. By the roads indeed the outside may be seen; but the footpaths go through the heart of the land."* Those are wise words. Even in a district you think you know well, you might be amazed at what you discover as you cross a stile on to a public footpath, or set out into the heart of a stretch of lonely moorland.

As a hobby rambling is inexpensive and can be done at any time throughout the year. You can walk through all the seasons of the year and in most weathers. Rambling can be enjoyed alone, with your family and friends, or in the good fellowship of a rambling club. If you like company it is a great way to make new friends.

This book is written for ramblers who are just discovering this most enjoyable of activities. But I hope more experienced country walkers might find something of value. It is intended to be an introduction, a starting point. Like the fingerpost that marks the footpath, a pointer in the right direction.

In its pages I will suggest places to walk, the gear you need (a modest investment compared to many hobbies), getting fit through rambling, the law concerning footpaths and bridleways, access to open countryside and trespass, solitary walking and joining a rambling group. There are some thoughts on hill and mountain walking, planning a walking tour and what to see when you are out in the countryside. It concludes by giving an account of some rambles that I have undertaken, which I hope will give you some thoughts on where you might go yourself, and views on aspects of rambling. Rambling doesn't need a great deal of preparation. It is all about just going out there and finding your feet. Enjoy your walks!

Chapter One: Finding Your Feet

When people think of ramblers, they usually picture walkers making their way across lonely stretches of countryside, tramping along coastal paths, or navigating across the wildest areas of Britain, our moorlands and mountains. The instant flash picture of a rambler in many people's imagination is someone fit with a large rucksack negotiating the Pennine Way. And, as a rambler, there is no reason why you can't walk in such wonderful locations.

But if you are an absolute beginner, it might be better to start somewhere closer to home. And don't imagine there is nowhere to walk but the streets if you are an urban dweller. Our cities and towns have sprawled quite widely during the past century, absorbing many ancient footpaths and bridleways. These can be sought out, along with canal towpaths and river banks. One of the finest walks in England is along the River Thames through the very urban heart of London. Public rights of way are marked on Ordnance Survey (OS) maps, even on sheets covering cities and towns. A number of rambling groups are based in urban areas and many have published books of urban walks. These are well worth seeking out. It is surprising how little many of us know about the places we grew up in.

If there is countryside close to home so much the better. Dig out the local OS map and go and find the footpaths and bridleways shown. Have a look in your local bookshop for books of walks – there is usually a guide available for most rural areas of Britain. If you are nervous about walking alone, then now is a good time to join your local rambling group. Local libraries and tourist information centres usually have a contact address.

One good idea is to walk the same walk at different seasons of the year, or even at different times of the day. It is quite surprising how things change over time. Sometimes it can almost appear to be a different countryside. Get to know your local paths like the back of your hand.

From such local beginnings you can walk further afield, driving or taking public transport to lonelier countryside. For example:

Long Distance Paths: Since the opening of the Pennine Way in the 1960s, a great profusion of long distance paths have been opened. Many have been adopted by government as National Trails, which suggests some measure and maintenance. The best knows, apart from the Pennine Way itself are: The Ridgeway Path, Offa's Dyke, the South Downs Way, the North Downs Way, the South West Coast Path, the Cotswold Way, the Pembrokeshire Coast Path, the Cleveland Way, The Thames Path and so on. There a very many less official long distance paths, such as the Two Moors Way in Devon, the Coast to Coast Path in northern England, the Cumbria Way, the Dales Way, the Teignmouth and Dawlish Way, and the Reivers Way and Rob Roy Way in Scotland. Scottish walkers can access the West Highland Way and several others. Guidebooks for all of these are available from bookshops and online. Many trails have their own supporting associations and it is worth visiting their websites before setting out. Please do note that many of these paths cross through wild countryside, so you really do need to be proficient with map and compass and be reasonably fit before setting out. Go walking locally first to build up the mileage you can cover and increase your stamina.

National Parks: Our National Parks offer some of the finest walking in Britain, with walks for people of all abilities. They are: Exmoor, Dartmoor, The New Forest, the South Downs, the Norfolk Broads, The Pembrokeshire Coast, the Brecon Beacons, Snowdonia, Peak District, Yorkshire Dales, North York Moors, Lake District,

Northumberland. So far Scotland has just two National Parks at Loch Lomond and the Trossachs, and the Cairngorms, though other areas are under consideration. Unlike some other countries, land in Britain's National Parks is usually privately owned. All of the National Parks have local societies as well as the official bodies that run them, and contact details for these groups can be found online. National Parks are ideal for longer walking breaks, but please learn how to read a map and use a compass. These are the wildest areas of Britain, with limited populations. Carry emergency food, drink and shelter before accessing their wildest areas, though most have gentler rambles, usually on their borders. Please don't walk beyond your ability and experience. All of the National Parks have websites, many with suggested walking routes.

Am I Fit Enough? It all depends what you intend to do. This book is no substitute for a proper medical examination. If you are reasonably fit then walking can only improve your fitness. I would stress that you certainly should not try to walk beyond your capabilities. If you have any medical conditions whatsoever then do consult your doctor before taking up rambling. Doctors generally recommend walking as good for the improvement of both physical and mental health. People with a wide range of ailments such as heart problems, diabetes, obesity, cancer, depression etc. have all been helped by walking. Rambling in the countryside is a good palliative for people with most mental health problems. There is further information on walking for health on the sites below. They are well worth a visit. Walking for Health gives details of health walks for the ill and unfit in most areas of Britain. The Ramblers offer short walks for beginners who may lack confidence. If in any doubt about whether or not rambling is right for *your* health problem then please do consult your doctor. http://www.walkingforhealth.org.uk/ and www.ramblers.org.uk

How Far Should I Walk? How far you walk in a day is up to you. Many ramblers who walk regularly do about 8 to 12 miles on an average ramble. Other ramblers do less than that. More determined walkers do up to 25 miles. If you like very long walks, consider joining the Long Distance Walkers Association. The LDWA has a most informative website http://www.ldwa.org.uk/ They have a number of local groups if you fancy some company. If you are new to rambling, it is better to do fewer miles than you suspect you are capable of, and really enjoy the walk, than be flagged out and miserable at the end of the day. There is no disgrace in walking just 4 or 5 miles. It is not the distance covered that matters, but the quality of the experience along the way. Many local groups of the Ramblers Association offer short and longer walks on their programmes. Rambling is not about going fast. It is about enjoying the walk, pausing when you feel like it, seeing the sights, sitting under a tree for a while to admire the view. I would only add that if you halt for too long on a strenuous walk, your muscles might stiffen when you get going again.

A good rule for the beginner is to work to a travelling pace of two and a half miles an hour, adding an hour for every 1500 feet of climb.

Many ramblers like to halt at a pub or café for a meal along the way. That is fine, but don't eat too heavily or you will feel the meal all the rest of the way. *If you are planning to halt in a pub or café, please bear in mind your muddy boots.* Leave them outside and within view, or put plastic bags over your boots before entering. Places of refreshment in well-known walking areas expect muddy and wet ramblers. In other areas they might not be so welcoming!

Walking Psychology Running out of steam on longer walks? Find a dozen miles daunting? Is it your ageing body protesting or is it all in the mind? Well, probably a bit of everything. I find I can't do the distances I did once. My longest was 68 miles in a day, but I was 20 and very fit at the time. I don't remember much about the last dozen miles. It wasn't a planned walk, just one of those interesting accidents where you just tag on a different finishing point. I wouldn't want to do it again, and realise it is nothing compared to those hardy members of the Long Distance Walkers Association who regularly top the 100. These days I prefer quality to quantity.

But I do think most people can walk more than they imagine. I have heard new ramblers exclaim that they couldn't do 10 miles? Well, I've said to them, you probably can, 10 or 20. Just think of the walk not the distance. Break the walk up. First 3 miles to some village, then another two miles up a hill, and so on. Don't dwell too much on the finish. And start early and finish later. Conditioned by wage slavery, many ramblers almost walk office hours, usually 10.30 to 4. Try starting at 8, or even earlier in the summer months, and finishing at 6. That way you can cover a good distance at a moderate pace. Don't be a slave to timings as though the office manager is on your back. I remember leading ~~victims~~ a walking group on a hot and dusty day. They were clearly tired. On their chinstraps as the military have it.

"How much further?" they groaned.

"A mile," I said.

With the end in sight they immediately perked up, chatting and lively, full of energy. It was, I confess, actually three miles, but the deceit served the purpose. They actually enjoyed the rest of the walk and finished with enthusiasm. Shakespeare, no mean walker, writes for Autolycus in *The Winter's Tale*:

Jog on, jog on the footpath way

And merrily hent the stile-a

Your merry heart goes all the way

Your sad tires in a mile-a.

A lot of truth in that. Grudge the distance ahead, dread the gradients, and where is the pleasure? Think of the walk and not the hard bits and the distance and you will love every minute.

Walking With Children: When I was young, children went rambling all on their own, or on expeditions with the Scouts and Guides. These days it has become a bit harder to coax the PlayStation™ generation out of doors. Yet most children love rambling when they are introduced to it as a family activity. There is no reason why children should not be taken on very short walks as soon as they can walk properly, as long as you recognise they might need to be carried, or that you need an easy escape route if it becomes too much for them. Then increase the distance as they grow older.

One of the best ways to enthuse young ramblers it to take them on walks with exciting features along the way, such as castles, hill forts, waterfalls. Give them plenty of time to look at the wildlife and farm animals. Encourage them to seek out animal tracks – handy to have a wildlife guide available. Try and explain some simple archaeology and geology as you pass through the land. Have plenty of stops in the most interesting parts of the walk, and let them look at your map, so they can see where they have been and what is to come. It is worth starting out in country parks or on marked nature trails, where there lots of opportunities for countryside interpretation. There are a number of guidebooks available detailing rambling routes suitable for children. Look in a local bookshop or online.

If they get the taste for country walking, then buy an appropriate rucksack, boots and clothing so that they might feel part of the rambling scene. As they get older, teach them some elementary navigation. Explain the differences between a footpath and a bridleway. Take them to farm open days, so that they might understand how the countryside works. Giving your children the freedom of their own land is a far better gift than the latest piece of technology.

Joining a Rambling Group

There are thousands of rambling groups across Britain, including local groups of The Ramblers (also known as the RA or Ramblers Association), groups independent but affiliated to the RA, and completely independent walking clubs. My personal belief is that all ramblers should join RA groups or at least affiliated clubs. For over seventy years the Ramblers Association has fought hard to save precious areas of our countryside, helped with the creation of our National Parks and National Trails, and fought for your right to walk in the countryside. By joining an RA group you are helping to support that valuable work.

The walks programmes of RA groups cater for all abilities and age groups (though they also have groups for younger members in their 20s and 30s in some areas if you so choose) and you will be sure of a warm welcome if you join. Most groups welcome prospective members for up to three walks to help you decide whether or not you wish to join. Groups often organise a wide variety of social events and even walking holidays. Some groups undertake voluntary activities such as waymarking and clearing footpaths, or writing walking guides.

Group members are very friendly and will usually give advice on places to walk or help you with map reading and compass work. Once you are an RA member you will have access to their map-lending library and receive their quarterly magazine *Walk* and a member's handbook You can use your membership card to obtain discounts at outdoor shops, places of interest etc. You can play as large or little a role in group activities as suits you. Look at their website on www.ramblers.org.uk

Groups That Every Rambler Should Join

The Ramblers Association – The RA, or The Ramblers as they prefer to be known these days, was born out of the access struggles of the 1930s, when the various Ramblers Federations of the day merged into a national association. Today, the RA promotes walking throughout mainland Britain, campaigns to protect footpaths and bridleways, fights for improved access to the countryside, and campaigns to protect our countryside. RA areas and groups organise thousands of walks every week, which members are free to go on. When you join you are assigned to your nearest group, though you may walk with any other RA group. It is in the best interests of every rambler to join the RA, whether you want to play an active role or just give nominal support. To join visit their website at www.ramblers.org.uk or write to The Ramblers, Camelford House, 87-90 Albert Embankment, London SE1 7TW. Telephone the RA membership team on 020 7339 8595 and they will enrol you there and then.

The Open Spaces Society – Britain's oldest national conservation group was founded in 1865. Its work is best described by its formal name, The Commons, Open Spaces and Footpaths Preservation Society. The OSS has a long and distinguished history fighting for all of the above. It tends to be the pace-setter of the access movement. It produces an informative magazine *Open Space*, runs training courses, is represented at public inquiries, and has a network of Local Correspondents who carry out OSS objectives in their particular areas. To join contact the Open Spaces Society at 25a Bell Street Henley-on-Thames RG9 2BA. Tel: 01491 573535 or Email: hq@oss.org.uk You can join online or download a membership application form at www.oss.org.uk

The Solitary Walker

A good many people enjoy walking alone, or perhaps with one other person. In some ways this is the best way to relate to nature and quietly enjoy the countryside. As long as you don't walk beyond your experience and abilities there is little danger in it. Don't be put off by scare stories. Our countryside is safe enough, safer in many instances than walking city streets. You can go at your own pace, stop when you want to, change your mind about your route. On that last point, some books on rambling suggest that the solitary walker should always "tell someone where they are going and when they expect to be back." Fair enough if you are nervous, or an absolute beginner. But I believe that is slavery for the more experienced rambler. If you learn how to navigate you should come to no harm. Take that map and compass out into a stretch of countryside you know really well and learn how to use them. It is not at all difficult. Many rambling groups, National Park Authorities, and local evening classes run courses on navigation for ramblers and hillwalkers. Residential course providers advertise in the Ramblers magazine *Walk* and other outdoor publications. If you have any doubts about your ability it is money well spent.

If being solitary is your thing, if you don't like the thought of walking with others in a group, then good for you. You will notice more about the countryside than most, see more wildlife, have time to really study antiquities and the lines of old trackways. Make the countryside your own by finding your feet. Walking alone, it becomes easier to talk to local people and get their perspective on where they live.

But I do believe that even the lone rambler should join the Ramblers Association and the Open Spaces Society. We all have a duty to protect the countryside, preserve its beauty and safeguard a right of access to it. A few quid for society memberships is a small enough contribution to make, even if you do nothing else in the way of volunteering.

Chapter Two: Walking Gear for the Beginner

If you believed some of the advertisements you see in outdoor magazines, you might think that rambling is a very expensive hobby. Believe me, it isn't. Like any other hobby you should buy the best you can afford. I started out paying next to nothing in army surplus stores. Shop around for walking gear as well as some stores are much cheaper than others. The one item of gear you shouldn't economise on is a good pair of walking boots and the walking socks that go in them. You will be on your feet all day, so you don't want them pinching or being too loose, or causing blisters. Go to a really good gear shop, get a proper fitting and go to the top of your personal budget. Look after them and they should give you a fair bit of use. So apart from boots and thick walking socks, what do you need?

It is lovely to look at old pre-war pictures of ramblers and see them nicely clogged out in tweeds, the gentlemen with ties and shorts or breeches, ladies in skirts. Perhaps we have lost something by moving so quickly into modern fibres. For lowland walking you don't need much more than comfortable casual clothing. One piece of advice. Avoid jeans. They are thoroughly miserable to wear once they get wet, clinging to and chafing the legs. Gear shops offer walking jackets and trousers at a range of prices so shop around. A good waterproof jacket (anything made of fabrics like Goretex™ is ideal as it repels rain but allows moisture from your body to evaporate). A pair of waterproof over-trousers are essential given the British climate, and a pair of gaiters, which will keep mud and water out of your boots on wet days – the best and easiest to use are those that fasten at the front. Some lowland walkers favour a waterproof poncho, which covers body and rucksack. They are fine, except on windy days. For hill and mountain walking you need to up your game. Gear for wintry conditions needs to be of a better quality. Seek advice from your local outdoor gear shop, but don't let them persuade you to buy the most expensive gear, unless money is no object to you.

So here is a list to start with:

Boots: The best you can afford. Go to a specialist gear shop and try several pairs until you find the most comfortable. Wear the kind of thicker walking socks you intend to use on actual walks. As our feet swell during the day, it is quite a good idea to buy boots in the afternoon. Walk around the shop to see how the boots feel. If there are stairs you can go up and down with the boots on, then so much the better. When you get the boots home, wear them round the house for a few hours so that you can see if they pinch or chafe. Some ramblers prefer walking shoes, though I prefer the cushioning and ankle support – and resistance you get to mud and water – that you get from boots. It is very much a personal choice and it is worth examining both possibilities when you are in a gear shop.

Socks: These are a matter of personal choice. I quite like the cushioning effect of thicker socks.

Rucksack: To start with you just need a reasonably sized daysack. Enough to pack away your waterproofs, maps, drink and lunch etc. If you intend to go on a walking tour or youth hostelling then you might need a bigger pack, but a daysack is the starting point. If you are planning to use trekking poles then, when they are not in use, you need a rucksack with outside straps to tie them on.

Clothing: See above, but it is best to dress in layers of clothes, so that you can put clothes on as you get cold and take them off as you get warm. For a short lowland walk, a showerproof jacket might do as a waterproof but if you are taking to the hills or undertaking a longer ramble, then go for the best waterproofs you can afford.

Temperatures can plunge in Britain, so some people pack a sweater (preferably wool) or a fleece in their rucksack.

Hats and Gloves: Many ramblers do not wear a hat at all, relying on the hoods of their walking jacket. Personally I like a hat at most times of the year. A broad-brimmed hat keeps the sun out of your eyes in hot weather, and much of the rain in wet. I use a Tilley® hat. They are virtually indestructible and are a worthwhile investment. I also wear a variety of tweed and cloth caps, plus a light sun-hat in a heat wave. Don't forget, on windy days you need to secure the hat or it will blow away. On cold days a pair of gloves or mitts (preferably thermal) are a good idea. You can get mitts which peel back to allow you to use your fingers, which is very useful.

Gaiters: These are very useful in muddy and wet weather, preventing mud and water getting into your boots. The best ones fasten up at the front which makes them easier to put on and off. In good dry weather you probably won't need them.

Compass: The Silva® type compass is the best for walking, as it includes a protractor so that you can take bearings. But do remember, a compass is not some lucky charm worn around the neck. You really do need to know how to use it and how to read maps. Some walkers these days also carry GPS devices, but they are no substitute for knowing how to read a map and use a compass.

Maps: The ideal for ramblers is the 1:25000 or roughly two and a half inches to the mile. These show field boundaries and – in England and Wales – footpaths and bridleways, which makes navigation a lot easier. The best maps for beginners are those produced by the Ordnance Survey, though some experienced hillwalkers favour Harvey's maps.

Refreshments: A flask of hot tea or coffee has a wonderful psychological effect as you come to the rest stop on your walk. Many walkers carry a cold drink as well, either in a water bottle or

Platypus, a plastic water container with a drinking tube. What you take to eat is up to you, but do remember that you will burn off a lot of calories as you walk, and these need to be replaced to give you energy.

First Aid Kit: A small first aid kit in a wallet, with a few basic essentials such as plasters, bandages, painkillers, blister plasters, antiseptic wipes etc. Most outdoor shops carry a selection.

Whistle: A very useful way to summon help in an emergency. Tie it on a strap so that it hangs inside your rucksack. Your whistle should really only be blown in an emergency. The international distress signal is six blasts on the whistle with a minute's gap in between.

Extras: Many walkers today carry a mobile telephone and a camera, binoculars (useful for route finding as well as watching wild creatures) notebooks etc. A foam sitmat to rest on while you are having your lunch is useful.

Walking Sticks/Trekking Poles: Whether you use a walking stick or trekking poles is a matter of personal choice. I favour a walking stick for easier walks and a pair of trekking poles for harder hillwalking. The latter are particularly useful on descents and help you to be more sure-footed on rough ground. Walking sticks and poles are useful as an aid to crossing streams, fending off unfriendly dogs and livestock and bashing down overgrowth on paths.

A Survival Bag: This sounds dramatic but it really is only a plastic bag you can crawl into in an emergency. Many ramblers only carry them for hillwalking or rambling off the beaten track. In my experience they rarely leave the bottom of the rucksack, but they are light enough and worth having.

Torch: It is a good idea to carry a torch, and not just in winter. A modern walker's headlamp is better than something you have to hold. If you are late back from a walk, it could prove a godsend.

Useful for signalling purposes in an emergency. Like the whistle signal, six flashes with a minute in between if you want to summon help.

Pedometer: These handy little devices, and quite cheap these days, tell you how many miles you have walked in a day.

Old Plastic Bag: This is for litter. Please take all of your litter back home with you, or at least to the first litter bin you come too. And that includes such things as banana skins which take a long time to rot down and are an unsightly evidence that humans came that way. Not only is litter a ghastly intrusion in our countryside, but wild creatures and farm animals regularly choke on it. No real rambler ever drops litter!

Walking Guides: Beginning ramblers often use walking guides, and there is a great abundance of them on the market, good, bad and indifferent. More experienced ramblers might use them for ideas and background information about places, but work out their own route from the map. Walking guides do play a useful service in that they encourage people to keep walking our footpaths and bridleways, helping to keep them open. Some walking guides have now been in print for many years, because they are definitive classic works of walking literature in their own right. Wainwright's beautifully drawn *Guides to the Lakeland Fells* are a case in point. First written in the 1950s they are still in use by fellwandering visitors to the Lake District. William Crossing's *Guide to Dartmoor* was first published in 1909, and should still be the first choice of wanderers on that wild moorland. Even after all the years that have passed since they were first written, you will know a lot about those districts if you carry out all of the walks therein. Perhaps, in the course of time, you will get to write a walking guide to an area you know.

Chapter Three: Rights of Way and Public Access

Public Rights of Way – A Brief Introduction to Paths and Countryside Access

England and Wales have a wonderful network of public footpaths and bridleways to enable you to access the countryside. Most of these paths have evolved over centuries and can lead you to some fascinating places. Footpaths and bridleways are public highways under law, just the same as other roads and you are legally entitled to walk upon them. The law also says that they should properly signposted, not obstructed and kept clear of growth. With a few exceptions only permitted traffic is allowed on them, such as:

Footpaths: These are available to walkers *only*.

Bridleways: May be accessed by walkers, horse-riders and bicycles.

Permissive Paths: Some landowners have opened up permissive paths. These are not rights of way, and you have no legal right to use them. You are there only under the tolerance of the landowner. They may be closed at any time.

BOATS (bridleways open to all traffic): These are essentially bridleways that may be accessed by motor vehicles, though unlike country lanes, they are essentially for walkers, riders and horse-drawn vehicles.

Questions about public rights of way

Can I stop for refreshments on a right of way? Yes, as long as you stay on the line of the path. That being said, most ramblers halt within a few yards of a right of way and most landowners don't mind.

Can I take a dog on a right of way? Yes, as long as it under close control at all times, and best on a lead where there is livestock. Remember that farmers have a legal right to shoot your dog if it is seen chasing livestock. To avoid spreading disease to farm animals, you should have your dog de-wormed regularly.

If the path is obstructed can I remove the obstruction? The law says that you can remove sufficient of the obstruction to allow you to pass, but you mustn't remove more than that or go out with the specific intention of clearing the path without permission. Please do note that before removing any obstruction you should make absolutely certain that you are on the *legal* line of the path, which might not necessarily be the exact line that people are walking. Check your map very carefully! Also note that wire fencing and barbed wire is usually held under great tension and may whip out if cut. Take great care! All obstructions should be reported to your local council and to the Ramblers (you can fill in an online report form on their website www.ramblers.org.uk) Local groups of the Ramblers and other groups regularly undertake permitted clearances of paths and welcome voluntary help. If in doubt let the highways authority deal with the obstruction.

What if crops are growing across the line of a path or it is ploughed up? If you are absolutely certain that you are on the line of a public right of way then you should make your way through. By going round the edge of the field instead you are trespassing and breaking the precept of the Country Code, which tells you to keep to the line of the path across farmland. Farmers and landowners have a legal obligation to keep rights of way clear of crops and to restore paths within a specified time after ploughing. If you come across such obstructions then do please report them to your local council and to the Ramblers.

Is mud an obstruction? Almost certainly not. The countryside is muddy and you have to live with it, walking out with good boots and gaiters. However, if there is any evidence that water or mud is being deliberately diverted across a path to deter users then there would be a case for obstruction. If water or excessive mud gathers on a right of way that you know, on a regular basis, then it is worth notifying the local highways authority and the Ramblers Association so that something can be done.

Are paths signposted? By law public rights of way should be signposted by fingerposts at the point where they leave a public road. Other waymarking along the route depends on the discretion of the landowner and the local highways authority, though it is in the interests of both to make it clear just where ramblers are supposed to be going.

A public right of way I know has a "Private" or "Keep Out" sign along its route? Report this to your local council and to the Ramblers. It is an offence to try to deter someone from using a public right of way.

What if I encounter a dangerous dog? If the dog is clearly being used to deter walkers then report it to your local council and the Ramblers. If it tries or succeeds in attacking you then report the incident at the nearest police station as soon as possible, as well as reporting to the local council and the Ramblers.

Should I always close gates? Always close gates that you have opened. If a gate is flapping in the wind, with the possibility that some other walker has left it open, then close it as well. If a gate has clearly been propped open then do please leave it alone. Do not do anything which would allow livestock to escape from a field. Locked gates that prevent you walking a path should always be reported to the local council and the RA.

Threatening landowner? Years ago, it was not uncommon to be challenged by a landowner when walking on a public right of way. Mostly they would deny there had any been a right of way anywhere near the one you were on. Thankfully it doesn't happen very much these days. Most farmers and landowners are welcoming, perhaps recognising that ramblers benefit the local economy. Should it happen to you, remember that the '*soft answer turneth away wrath*' or whatever. Get your map out and show the landowner where you think you are and point out the line of the right of way. Listen to what he says. You might be wrong. He might be right. Or the other way round. The path may have been diverted since your map was printed or closed altogether. Keep both your blood pressures low if you can. If you are absolutely sure you were on the line of the right of way, then please do report the matter to your local highways authority and to the Ramblers Association.

A footbridge, stile or fingerpost sign was missing on a path I walked? Report the missing item, with a map reference and/or a clear description to the local council, and to the Ramblers Association.

Can paths be diverted or closed? Yes, they can, but only by proper statutory order, not because a landowner decides to do so off their own bat. The local highways authority will have Definitive Map of Public Rights of Way, which should be open to public examination by appointment. This will tell you the current status of any footpath or bridleway.

I know a path that has always been a right of way but it is not on the map? The fact that a right of way isn't on the Ordnance Survey map or the local Definitive Map doesn't make it any less of a right of way. It has probably not been claimed by anyone. If you can prove twenty years use, in any period of time, without obstruction, or notices saying you are walking only by permission of the landowner, then you can try claiming the path and getting it put on the Definitive Map of Public Rights of Way. If you know of such a path then it is worth seeking advice on how to make a claim from the Ramblers Association or the Open Spaces Society.

I am a landowner and would like to create new rights of way on my land? Please do! Contact the Ramblers Association or Open Spaces Society for advice.

Trespassing: England and Wales do not have the general access enjoyed in Scotland. Walk away from public rights of way or access land and you are trespassing. But the "Trespassers Will Be Prosecuted" signs you see here and there are pretty meaningless in law. With some exceptions, trespassing in England and Wales is a tort, a civil offence and not a criminal offence. Which means you can't be prosecuted, unless you cause damage. Trespass *is* a criminal offence if you trespass in places like the royal estates, military training grounds and establishments, and railways etc.

Should you cause damage, the landowner might sue you in the civil courts. But it would have to be a proven and measurable damage. Simply walking through a woodland track or bending down a bit of grass probably wouldn't count, and certainly wouldn't be worth suing for, though you could be liable for the landowner's legal costs if they wanted to take the gamble. However, if you force your way through a hedgerow, break a gate or damage a fence etc., the landowner might be able to claim damages. If your actions cause livestock to roam and an animal is lost or injured then the damages could be considerable. Please bear this in mind before deciding to wander away from rights of way.

Landowners also have a right in law to physically remove you from their land, though only if they use *reasonable force*. If they challenge you, they can insist that you leave their land forthwith. But they can only make you go to the nearest public highway; i.e. road, footpath, bridleway etc. These are just very brief guidance notes on trespassing and should not be taken as legal definitions. Please consult the Blue Book (see the next paragraph) if you want an absolutely definitive ruling on trespassing matters. As I understand the law, you are not obliged to give a landowner your name and address.

The above comments are a very brief introduction to path law and land access in England and Wales and the comments made above are a guide only. If you want a more detailed explanation then please do visit the Ramblers website at www.ramblers.org.uk The classic book on rights of way law is what is called 'the Blue Book' its title being *Rights Of Way: a guide to law and practice* published jointly by the Ramblers and the Open Spaces Society. If you are interested in footpath work and your right to walk it is the one to get and it is usually accepted as the definitive answer to any legal matter.

Footpath work: If you are interested in helping to keep open public rights of way, then do please consider doing voluntary work for the Ramblers Association and the Open Spaces Society. Rambling groups often need new footpath officers. You can do no greater service for present and future walkers and riders.

Freedom to Roam: In addition to the public paths network you have a legal right to roam (in England and Wales) under the *Countryside and Rights of Way Act 2000* – commonly known as CRoW - on uncultivated mountain and moorland, common land, heath and downland. In addition some Forestry Commission forests and National Nature Reserves have been added. Some landowners have dedicated land as access land under the Act. Such areas may be closed by landowners for up to 28 days per year so please check locally. Access land is marked by a yellow wash on Ordnance Survey maps. The Ramblers Association is currently campaigning for complete access to the English Coast (It already exists in Wales). There is a long way to go, so please support them in their campaign.

Access in Scotland: The Scottish land access situation is very different to that in England and Wales. The *Land Reform Act (Scotland) 2003* gives walkers a near absolute legal right to roam, except in certain cases, such as away from the gardens and immediate policies of houses and some government land. Paths tend not to be shown in the same way on Ordnance Survey maps. But there are rights of way in Scotland and a number of walking trails. If you walk at all in Scotland then please support ScotWays (the Scottish Rights of Way and Access Society) and Ramblers Scotland. Both have very useful websites which gives a great deal of information on access, paths to walk and suggested routes. Visit their websites at: www.scotways.com and www.ramblers.org.uk/scotland/ For information on the Scottish Access Code please visit http://www.outdooraccess-scotland.com/

Ireland: While there seems to be *de facto* access to the more popular walking areas of Ireland, tales abound of restrictions and downright hostility from some farmers and landowners. For further information please visit the website of Mountaineering Ireland at http://www.mountaineering.ie If you are Irish or visit Ireland please support their campaigns for improved access. The Irish and Northern Ireland tourist boards have lots of information on walking routes and accommodation. However, there are a number of walking guides to Eire and Northern Ireland, so I presume that the walking routes therein are okay to walk.

Why We Should Preserve The Original Lines Of Our Rights Of Way

The original lines of our ancient pathways should be preserved, not only that we might find access to the heart of our countryside, but so that we might do so in the footsteps of our ancestors. Britain's network of public footpaths and bridleways might be eccentric to the bureaucratic eye, but it does serve a good purpose as a way of accessing the land without trespassing.

We are fortunate that there are so many footpaths and bridleways – the first the domain of walkers only, the latter that of walkers, cyclists and horse riders. These are now marked on the Ordnance Survey maps and on the Definitive Maps of rights of way kept by local authorities. They are, in law, part of the Queen's Highway, just the same as a country lane, urban road or motorway. But our rights of way network is probably the most undervalued, certainly the most underfunded, recreational resource in Britain, given that it is open to all. These paths offer excitement and adventure, often hidden behind a stile or shooting gate.

In a delightful little essay on footpaths, the Victorian country writer Richard Jefferies entices us in the exploration of these old paths " 'always get over a stile' is the one rule that should be borne in mind by those who wish to see the land as it really is – that is to say, never omit to explore a footpath, for never was there a footpath yet which did not pass something of interest."

How did such a delightful and often quirky network of paths come about? Fortunately these old routes were not designed by bureaucrats, emerging with, at best, the tacit approval of landowners and authority. Paths were forged around our landscape by people, which is why we have ancient ridgeways across the landscape's highest ground, mostly in use for thousands of years. Routes were defined by the need to avoid marsh and dense woodland.

Here are the ways taken by our prehistoric ancestors as they journeyed for trade with neighbouring tribes or to the sea in search of salt. In the centuries that followed the ridgeways facilitated the movement of armies. In Saxon times Alfred the Great defeated the Danish invaders by his knowledge of paths that were aged even in his time. Drovers moved their animals to market along wild and lonely drove routes, their fires burning like beacons in the night as they rested at traditional stopping places. To follow a ridgeway, as many walkers and riders do today, is to walk in the very footsteps of British history.

We have paths that follow the sections of Roman roads bypassed by modern roadmenders, green lanes wind through our forests and pastoral landscapes, some sunk deep into hollow ways with the tread of generations of passers-by. In the vicinity of towns and villages might be found the paths along which our rural ancestors travelled to church or local markets.

Here are the wider ways that once echoed to the horns of stage coaches in those heady days before motor traffic demanded straighter routes. Such paths are an important part of our social heritage and should never be taken for granted. They are as much a part of Britain's story as our village churches and prehistoric monuments.

Yet there are those who want this quaint and important network sanitised, revised and destroyed. Some landowners remain hostile to these outlets for recreation and access. Landowning organisations persist in seeking to have the rights of way network "rationalised". Council bureaucrats seek to stamp their unimaginative control over the idea of any paths that do not fit into their brief of easily-controlled and inexpensive "recreational routes". Why, they argue, would anyone really want to walk the way that local people went to church, or in the footsteps of medieval pilgrims or cattle drovers? Why not straighten the paths, divert them round the edges of the fields they pass through and steer them away from farming hamlets? Why not close some paths altogether?

These arguments should always be resisted. We should no more tolerate the destruction of our historic rights of way network than we would the crashing down of Stonehenge or the Tower of London. Do we really want to be the last generation capable of walking in the footsteps of our ancestors?

It is the duty of all of us to preserve Britain's rights of way network for future generations. Our ancient paths are worth fighting for. Please do all you can to help.

Freedom to Roam

I make no apology for being a rambling campaigner for the right to roam. Surely every rambler should seek as much access to his or her homeland as possible. As John Stuart Mill wrote, as long ago as 1848: *No man made the land, it is the original inheritance of the whole species. The land of every country belongs to the people of that country.*

And yet the people of Britain are denied access to many of the finest landscapes of their own country. We live in a strange land, where we are but subjects not citizens. Where it is deemed honourable for our young men and women to *die* for their country, but heaven help them if they want to walk across much of it. Worth remembering too, that some landowners are acquiring tens of thousands of pounds each year of your money, public money, the tax we have to pay – often equivalent to a lottery win – in subsidies. At a time when government is slashing pensions and the welfare budget for the majority.

There have been victories. The *2000 Countryside and Rights of Way Act* gave us the right to roam on mountain, moorland, downland, heath and common. Even now organisations such as the Ramblers Association are fighting to get the British people access to our coastline - surely an inalienable right for an island nation.

But England and Wales are poorly served compared to Scotland, where recent legislation gives people the right to roam *everywhere* with very limited exceptions, such as the immediate gardens and policies of people's homes, or through areas of growing crops. This is the kind of generous legislation that we need in the rest of Britain.

Years ago the Ramblers Association ran a *Forbidden Britain* campaign. Perhaps it is time the Forbidden Britain campaign was revived. Some areas are much more difficult to access than others. Such as:

Forbidden Woodlands: Britain's woodlands are the landscapes most denied to the people of our country, their glades the backdrop to most of the conflicts between landowners and the landless. On many rural walks you will encounter every permutation of *Keep Out* and *No Trespassing* signs, warning of dire consequences if you stray from lane and path and attempt to enter these green havens. It was not always so. A couple of centuries ago local inhabitants would wander quite freely through the greenwood, gathering nuts fallen from the trees, and dead wood for their cottage fires. Vast areas of woodland and forest are still out of bounds to the most innocent of country walkers.

The very principle of enclosure and restrictions of access to land, especially woodland, set aside for game preservation has been challenged from its very beginning. By the nineteenth century the war against exclusive ownership of the land had begun, fuelled partly by the need of the poor actually to survive and the increasing use of rural areas for leisure pursuits. Such was the scale of this predation upon property rights that by 1878 the country essayist Richard Jefferies described it from the landowners' view as 'a great grievance'. In an article for *The Livestock Journal* Jefferies complained that:

the value of property has enormously increased, but the legal protection in respect of trespass has not marched with the age…a fine of a shilling, after days of trouble with solicitors and witnesses, is simply a ridiculous remedy, not to mention the difficulty of identifying trespassers when time has elapsed. It is hardly too much to say, that a man with two or three pounds in his pocket to pay nominal damages and fines, might walk across a country just where he chose, provided he did not get too close to dwelling houses, and come within the charge of being on premises for an unlawful purpose. The alternative of proceeding for trespass in a superior court is so expensive, protracted, and uncertain, as to be practically inoperative, except when great questions of right are involved. The whole question of trespass, in short, demands the early and the serious consideration of Parliament.

Richard Jefferies had rather a bipolar view of countryside access. As the son of a small farmer, and a journalist contributing to the Tory press, he might hold up his hands in horror at anything that smacked of socialism and an attack on property rights. But as a country-goer, not unsympathetic to poaching and country walking, he could see the other side of the coin, and he was to adopt a more radical outlook on social issues in the years before his premature death.

His earliest country books, *The Gamekeeper at Home* and *The Amateur Poacher* examine in a most interesting way the frustrations caused by enclosure and game preservation. In *The Gamekeeper at Home*, woodland trespassers are listed with predatory animals, poachers and vermin as the gamekeeper's *enemies*, whether they are the local poor gathering nuts, firewood and branches to make walking sticks, or the newly-urbanised visitor:

The keeper thinks that these trespassers grow more coarsely mischievous year by year. He can recollect when the wood in a measure was free and open, and, provided a man had not got a gun or was not suspected of poaching, he might roam pretty much at large; while the resident labouring people went to and fro by the nearest short cut they could find.

This gamekeeper of Burderop Wood in Wiltshire had unusual recollections in this case or was misleading Jefferies with an extremely biased viewpoint. Game was rigorously preserved in most southern woods throughout the nineteenth century and both poachers and walkers were severely discouraged. In his portrait of the gamekeeper, Jefferies tells us that the he and his underlings would shake immature nuts off trees to daunt locals from entering the wood for nutting. And for all his words about the halcyon days of freer access, Jefferies records the presence of an ancient man trap in the keeper's cottage:

In a dark corner there lies a singular-looking piece of mechanism, a relic of the older times, which when dragged into the light turns out to be a man trap. These terrible engines have long since been disused – being illegal, like spring-guns – and the rust has gathered thickly on the metal. But, old though it be, it still acts perfectly, and can be 'set' as well now as when in bygone days poachers and thieves used to prod the ground and the long grass, before they stepped in it, with a stick, for fear of mutilation.

The trap is almost precisely similar to the common rat trap or gin still employed to destroy vermin, but greatly exaggerated in size, so that if stood on end it reaches to the waist, or above. The jaws of this iron wolf are horrible to contemplate – rows of serrated projections, which fit into each other when closed, alternating with spikes a couple of inches long, like tusks. To set the trap you have to stand on the spring – the weight of a man is about sufficient to press it down; and, to avoid danger to the person preparing this little surprise, a band of iron can be pushed forward to hold the spring while the catch is put into position, and the machine itself is hidden among the bushes or covered with dead leaves. Now touch the pan with a stout walking stick – the jaws cut it in two in the twinkling of an eye. They seem to snap together with a vicious energy, powerful enough to break the bone of the leg; and assuredly no man ever got free whose foot was once caught by those terrible teeth.

A few years ago, I visited a manor house on the edge of Dartmoor and was shown just such a man trap, a vicious looking engine that could only have been intended to maim any poor unfortunate who got caught in its mighty jaws. For weeks afterwards, as I roamed unheeded around the estate's several hundred acres of woodland, the thought occurred to me that there might be other man traps, long since lost in the undergrowth surrounding its ancient oaks, but still set and waiting to crush the leg of a passing trespasser.

In the earlier years of the nineteenth century, every walk in the countryside must have been fraught with danger from such well-placed man traps and spring guns. The most likely victim of these 'terrible engines' was not the skilled local poacher, who would be wary and knowledgeable when entering the preserved park and its wooded coverts, but the naturalist on the lookout for specimens, the literary gentleman seeking inspiration, the early rambler and, most likely of all, the local labourer and his family desperate for firewood, nuts and mushrooms. The contemporary writer and social commentator Sydney Smith declared in the pages of *The Edinburgh Review* that 'there is a sort of horror in thinking of a whole land filled with lurking engines of death…'

Even on my country walks from the 1960s onwards, it was not unusual to find warning signs threatening dire misfortune if you dared to stray off the road or public path. The favourite bore the *caveat* 'Beware of Snakes', often adding for good measure the telephone number of the local hospital. Other notices threatened that, if you trespassed, you would be 'prosecuted with the full force of the law' or that 'severe civil and criminal action would be taken against you'. There were still spring guns in some of the game preserves, designed to go off if you knocked into a trip wire, albeit just to send off a warning shot to the landowner or keeper rather than putting a dose of lead into your leg. I have never, personally, encountered any man traps, but there is some anecdotal evidence that a small minority of landowners were still setting them or putting about the rumour that they were, well into the twentieth-century.

But the desire to roam is fundamental to human nature. There will always be a minority who will never accept that they may not go where they will. In his delightful book *The Amateur Poacher*, Richard Jefferies positively revels in the idea of trespass, albeit in the illicit pursuit of game. An examination of his many writings shows that he must have walked, with or without permission, through much of the countryside of Wiltshire and Sussex. He loathed any sort of work on his father's tiny farm and was never happier than when free to roam around the countryside. And for all his legitimate wanderings through Burderop Park in the company of its gamekeeper, there must have been illicit trespassing as well prompting Burderop's owner to comment that young Jefferies was 'not the sort of fellow you want hanging about in your coverts'.

Both Burderop Wood and the fields around Jefferies' home at Coate were very near the growing Victorian railway town of Swindon. With the growth of industry many workers, perhaps dispossessed agricultural labourers and their descendants, sought out the countryside in their limited leisure hours, coming into contact and conflict with the restrictions imposed by country landowners. Some of these expeditions would be in search of a rabbit or bird for the pot, perhaps a legacy of a more rural upbringing, but even amongst the working class there was a growing interest in education and natural history, and country rambling was a form of liberation in itself.

Elizabeth Gaskell gets the feeling of this new working class leisure activity in her novel *Mary Barton*, when she writes of labourers near Manchester who '...deafened with noise of tongues and engines, may come to listen awhile to the delicious sounds of rural life.' While in her novel she refers to workers following a footpath, many more would have roamed freely across the land, particularly in the vicinity of the growing Victorian towns and cities, adding to the conflict between the landed and the landless.

The rural poor who were hanging on to life in that same countryside struggled to survive, continuing, where they might, to use the woods and meadows as a source of food and materials for basic survival. But as increasing numbers of country and town dwellers sought out Britain's open spaces for existence and pleasure, so landowners intensified their efforts to create no-go areas to keep these interlopers out of their private pleasure grounds. Whole villages found themselves cut off from ancient sources of supply.

The naturalist W.H. Hudson tells of a typical land conflict in his book *A Shepherd's Life*, relating how a Wiltshire woman, Grace Reed, took on the earls of Pembroke over the right to gather wood in the forests around Wilton:

It will be readily understood that this right possessed by the people of two villages, both situated within a mile of the forest, has been a perpetual source of annoyance to the noble owners in modern times, since the strict preservation of game, especially of pheasants, has grown to be almost a religion to the landowners...about half a century or longer ago, the Pembroke of that time made the happy discovery...that there was nothing to show that the Barford people had any right to the dead wood. They had been graciously allowed to take it, as was the case all over the country at that time, and that was all. At once he issued an edict prohibiting the taking of dead wood from the forest by the villagers, and great as the loss was to them they acquiesced...not a man dared to disobey the prohibition or raise his voice against it.

Grace Reed then determined to oppose the mighty earl, and accompanied by four other women of the village went boldly to the wood and gathered their sticks and brought them home. They were summoned before the magistrates and fined, and on their refusal to pay were sent to prison; but the very next day they were liberated and told that a mistake had been made, that the matter had been inquired into, and it had been found that the people of Barford did really have the right they had exercised so long to take dead wood from the forest.

Hudson states:

As a result of the action of these women the right has not been challenged since, and on my last visit to Barford...I saw three women coming down from the forest with as much dead wood as they could carry on their heads and backs. But how near they came to losing their right!"

Forbidden Downland: One of the great disasters of the *Countryside and Rights of Way Act 2000* was that the amount of Downland that got mapped was very limited. The intention of the Act was to give a right to roam across many of our Downs. It didn't happen! Many areas of Downland were excluded because of the way that had been farmed in recent decades.

Forbidden Rivers: The Scottish access legislation gives walkers the right to access rivers, both on foot along the banks, and, where practicable on the waters themselves, by way of swimming, boats, canoes and kayaks. In England and Wales we are not so fortunate. Many miles of English and Welsh rivers have no access whatsoever.

Forbidden Moorland: Although much moorland and mountain was mapped as access land under the CRoW Act in 2000, some areas were missed and still need fighting for. Some areas of moorland were excluded because the landowners had carried out very minimal agricultural practices on them. The look like moorland but, because of poor drafting of the Act, they are excluded.

Forbidden Coastline: A few years ago, Parliament legislated for a continuous coastal path around England and Wales (the *Marine and Coastal Access Act 2009*). The Welsh sections are now open. But much of the English coast is still awaiting the creation of a continuous path and accompanying access areas. The Ramblers Association is campaigning hard for this so please lend them you support and lobby your MP and local councillors, if you live close to the coast.

Groups like the Ramblers and the Open Spaces Society are always campaigning to increase access to the countryside. Why not help them by volunteering or at least joining as a member?

Chapter Four: Hillwalking and the Walking Tour

Hillwalking: If you are completely new to rambling, then I would suggest you get in a few months low-level rambles before heading for Britain's wildest countryside – the moorlands, fells, hills and mountains. You need a degree of confidence and personal fitness if you are building up from scratch. Hillwalking (they call it fellwalking in the north of England) demands a great deal of energy. A long day of very steep ascents and descents can really take it out of you if you are unfit. You need to be able to cover a lot more mileage. So do build up gradually. Add a mile or two each time you go out for a low-level ramble.

You need to really be able to navigate with a map and compass. Okay, you might be ace with a Satnav and they are very handy items of kit to have, but map and compass first. If the batteries of the Satnav fail or the whole instrument packs up, then you could be in trouble. Time and again I hear stories of people phoning Mountain Rescue groups on their mobile phones so that they can ask the way. *This not what our very stretched Mountain Rescue groups are for!*

There are a great many books available on using map and compass (I have suggested a couple in the Recommended Books section below). Buy one today – even if you want to ramble in pastoral countryside – and practice, practice, practice. Work at it until you can do it in your sleep. Learn to take bearings across open country until you can really find the smallest navigational feature, such as a footbridge or an antiquity. Learn to take back-bearings, resections etc. Know the differences between true north, magnetic north and grid north. Learn how to find your position using a map and compass. Learn how to set the map, read contours, work out grid references, and so on. It sounds a lot but it is not difficult. Only then, when you feel competent, should you take to the hills.

I don't want to give the impression that country walks, even hill walks, are one long procession where you are doing little else than staring at a map and compass, rather than the delightful countryside. I rarely even look at a compass, except on days of poor visibility. I have spent so much time with maps that I have learned not only to read them but the landscape as well. With experience, you learn to *see* the landscape from a preliminary examination of the map, gaining a fair idea of what the countryside on your walk will look like. You back this up with a glance every now and again, to check your position, particularly when you are about to change course. Then you can really enjoy the countryside you are walking through.

If this all sounds complicated or you are not absorbing what you read, then seek help. If you join a rambling group you will usually find someone who will teach you the basics. Some local authorities run evening classes in navigation, as do some National Park authorities. If you have a few pounds to spare, then consider going on a navigation course. You will find advertisements for these in all the national walking magazines. You can do a basic course in a day or weekend, or enrol in a longer course which will turn you into a budding Ray Mears or Bear Grylls. Best to do a course in a hill or mountain area.

Some of these courses also include the basic elements of weather forecasting. You don't need a degree in meteorology to go hillwalking, but it helps to know what the weather is going to do before you get out into the wide open spaces. Despite what it might say on a television or radio weather forecast, mountain country tends to make its own weather. It can be very pleasant in a Scottish glen but there might be near arctic conditions on the top of a nearby mountain range. Fortunately, a number of online and telephone weather forecasts have become available for hillwalkers. Try the Mountain Weather Information Service at www.mwis.org.uk Most National Park and Tourist Information Centres, Youth Hostels etc. in hill districts will provide you with a local weather forecast if you ask.

Experienced hillwalkers go hillwalking in all weathers. If you are a beginner it is best to go out when the weather is at its best. In winter, when there is ice and snow on the ground, there is no such thing as hillwalking in our mountain districts. It is *mountaineering* and calls on a great deal of experience and stamina. It is beyond the scope of this book. Get in a good season's spring to autumn hillwalking before you attempt it. Then go with an experienced group, or enrol on a winter mountaineering course.

This book is about rambling, not rock climbing or hard scrambling. Keep off cliffs and craggy mountain slopes until you have experience. Then seek guidance and instruction. You can get to the summits of most of Britain's mountains without actual rock climbing. Get some practice on these easier (not always that easier) ascents before going up by the harder routes. Britain has a great many climbing instructors and climbing schools, who advertise in the outdoor press. Seek them out if you want to learn to rock climb or scramble.

On a long hill walk, you need to carry more food and drink. You will be burning calories to a much faster degree than you would on a low-level ramble. If you don't want your energy level to drop, leaving you tired out, you need to refuel. Think carbohydrates, proteins etc. No harm in having some emergency rations in your rucksack, such as chocolate, fruit nuts or the famous Kendal Mint Cake – just in case you get caught out or benighted.

Similarly, you need to carry more kit. A plastic survival bag that you can crawl into in an emergency is a must. Better wet weather gear, spare warm clothing and socks are a good idea too. I always like to carry a spare compass in the bottom of my rucksack in case I lose or break the one I'm using. It is no bad idea, if you are hillwalking in remote areas, to have a relevant spare map.

Should you need to call out Mountain Rescue, either for yourself or someone else, dial 999 or 112 and ask for the Police, then for Mountain Rescue. Try to give an accurate map reference and description for your present position, and explain why you need help. If you are calling on a mobile phone (and there is no point in taking one on a walk unless it is fully charged), give them your number and leave the phone on, so that the Rescue Controller can call you back. Once you have made the call, *stay exactly where you are.* Don't wander off unless you need to walk a *short* distance to get a better mobile phone signal. If you have any fluorescent clothing or a survival bag put it out so that you become easier to see. Try and keep as warm as possible. Please Remember that Mountain Rescue is for serious incidents only!

All that being said, the majority of hillwalkers go through a lifetime of hillwalking without ever having anything go wrong. I would repeat, become an expert at navigation and go well-equipped. It is a good idea to start hillwalking by following a guide book for routes. These abound in local bookshops, and will help you picture your route before you set off.

The Walking Tour: Once you have built up some experience of rambling, there is nothing better than exploring these beautiful islands on a walking tour. In days of yore I used to wander for weeks on end around parts of Britain; often with a tent, sometimes from youth hostel to youth hostel, and now and again sleeping out. A walking tour gives you the opportunity to explore some of Britain's long distance paths, such as the Coast to Coast Walk or the Dales Way. Or follow in the footsteps of medieval pilgrims on some of the old pilgrimage routes. Or walk a great river such as the Thames, from its source to where it meets the sea. Many stretches of our coastline have coastal paths you can follow. See chapter one for some suggestions.

Don't underestimate the physical and psychological challenge of walking day after day. If you are not used to continuous walking it can take it out of you. Better not to try to do too many miles in a day and have occasional rest days. Before attempting longer routes such the Pennine Way or the West Highland Way, it is far better to try one of the shorter paths. Or make up your own route for a weekend's tramp. Bear in mind that you will be carrying more kit than on a day's ramble, especially if you intend to camp out. Get used to carrying this heavier load on some of your day rambles before your great expedition. But do try to travel as light as possible.

You will, of course, need to stay overnight on your walking tour. This can either mean camping out or staying bed and breakfast or in a youth hostel, or a combination of all three. Camping is beyond the remit of this book. But there are many books on backpacking for the tyro tramper. It is worth joining the Backpackers Club for information, even if you don't intend to join in their club meets. Visit their website at http://www.backpackersclub.co.uk/

Sadly, the great network of youth hostels that I used to enjoy visiting, years ago, walking from one to the next, has retracted in most areas of Britain. But they are still useful where they do exist and are worth staying in as a change from a b & b. Visit their website at http://www.yha.org.uk/ to find out how to become a member (you don't have to be a youth!) and for locations. The YHA also run useful hillwalking and navigation classes based at hostels. There are a number of independent hostels, camping barns and bothies in some walking areas. Look at the Independent Hostels website at http://www.independenthostelsuk.co.uk/

The Mountain Bothies Association http://www.mountainbothies.org.uk/ maintains simple bothies in hill districts, if you fancy more Spartan tramping. Their website is well worth visiting and offers a location map.

Many ramblers stay in bed and breakfast establishments as they wander from village to village. These vary in price, but they do offer a cooked breakfast and the chance to have a shower or bath. Some will provide packed lunches. Accommodation that caters for ramblers can be sought out on an excellent accommodation finder on the Ramblers website www.ramblers.org.uk or try local tourist information boards. It is worth noting that accommodation on the more popular walking routes tends to book up very quickly, so consider booking in advance.

If you don't want to go alone on your walking tour, some walking holiday firms organise walking tour holidays in Britain and abroad. Try Ramblers Holidays at http://www.ramblersholidays.co.uk/ or the Holiday Fellowship at http://www.hfholidays.co.uk/ The Youth Hostels Association also organises walking trips based at their hostels at http://www.yha.org.uk

Whilst many of the long distance trails are waymarked where they cross lower ground, do bear in mind that you will often have to navigate with a map and compass on the hills and across moorland. Please make sure you are competent and fit before setting out.

The joy of the walking tour, like the pleasure of the day ramble, is that you get the chance to see parts of Britain that most Britons never see. In the words of the nineteenth-century tramper and writer George Borrow, in his book *The Romany Rye*: "*On I went on my journey, traversing England from west to east, ascending and descending hills, crossing rivers by bridge and ferry, and passing over extensive plains. What a beautiful country is England! People run abroad to see beautiful countries, and leave their own behind unknown, unnoticed – their own the most beautiful! And then again, what a country for adventures! Especially to those who travel on foot, or on horseback."*

Walking the Two Moors Way: Why not walk the Two Moors Way, the long-distance path crossing Dartmoor, mid-Devon and Exmoor? A 100 mile plus journey into Devon's quieter hinterlands, the Two Moors Way is a wonderful way to see some of the best of the West Country's scenery. It is also one of the better long-distance paths for less experienced ramblers. That said, the route shouldn't be taken for granted. There is some rough moorland walking in the National Parks, and you need to be fit and proficient with a map and compass.

The idea for a path across Devon was first mooted in the 1970s by Sylvia Sayer (Dartmoor Preservation Association), John Coleman-Cooke (Exmoor Society) and Tom Stephenson (of Ramblers and Pennine Way fame). The original idea was for a bridleway, but that concept – and much of their suggested route – was ditched in the face of massive landowner resistance. In despair, the Devon Ramblers Association turned to its renowned member, the late Joe Turner, to devise a route using existing rights of way and areas of *de facto* access. The Two Moors Way that people enjoy today is testimony to Joe Turner's vision and real hard work.

In a sense, the Dartmoor and Exmoor sections were easy, with a long tradition of public access. The pastoral lands of mid-Devon were not so easy. Some of the rights of way simply didn't exist at all on the ground, or were completely blocked. I remember going out surveying routes with Joe in the early 70s. We found a complete lack of signposting, green lanes blocked completely with hundreds of fallen trees, missing stiles, gates and bridges, baffled farmers who had never set eyes on a rambler before. It seemed a nightmare to me, perhaps 70% of the projected route unwalkable.

But Joe Turner didn't give up!

In just a couple of years, he had those paths signposted and cleared, stiles and bridges built. Joe's personal charm and character had won over an initially suspicious farming community, to the extent that farmers were actually suggesting where new link paths might be created. By the time a guidebook was published, written by the late Helen Rowett, the route was opened.

And what a route it is! Starting from Ivybridge, the TMW climbs into the lonely uplands of southern Dartmoor, through very wild moorland, where your only company might be sheep and skylarks. Then down into the valley of the Dart at New Bridge, before climbing out on to the great ridge of Hameldown. More moorland brings the walker to the Teign Gorge, and to Drewsteignton, where Dartmoor is left behind.

The next 32 miles cross the pastoral fields and woodlands of mid-Devon, through some enchanting villages, passing ancient churches and cob cottages, before entering the Exmoor National Park near to West Anstey. Then a walk across high moorlands and deep combes, alongside great rivers such as the Barle and the Exe. The final descent to the finish at Lynmouth is one of the most spectacular walks in southern England.

The Two Moors Way has been a great success story, with walkers coming from all over the world to explore its picturesque miles. The guide book has been a bestseller for nearly forty years, and the Two

Moors Way brings millions of pounds a year into the local economy, keeping open many a pub, shop and bed and breakfast establishment.

And as you walk the Two Moors Way, remember Joe Turner, whose commitment and hard work – along with those of his wife Pat – made this walk possible, giving such great joy to the tens of thousands who have followed in his footsteps. Joe's name will forever be associated with this remarkable, quiet and lovely long distance trail. *The Official Guide to The Two Moors Way, by Helen Rowett, published by the Two Moors Way Association and Devon County Council is by far the best guide, and available from good bookshops and online retailers.*

Chapter Five: What To See On Walks

Rambling is not usually an end in itself. The act of walking through the countryside gives you an opportunity to explore the land itself through other interests. The story of the land, the antiquities and buildings upon it, and the way people live and have lived, is endlessly fascinating. There are more things to do and know about than you could possibly achieve in an average lifespan. Rambling allows you to become an expert in one or more, or a dabbler, curious about everything.

You can certainly get more pleasure from rambling by interpreting the land itself, its geology, archaeology and history. Professor W.G. Hoskins' grand book *The Making of the English Landscape* is the place to start. It is very readable and aimed at the general reader rather than the specialist. Every country walker should read it as a starting point. You will never look at the English landscape in the same way again. There are other specialist works about the other countries of the British Isles – a search in bookshops or on the internet will show you the most appropriate ones for your country and interests.

Ancient Tracks: A particularly good hobby for the rambler is to make a study of the paths and tracks you are walking along. How they came to be there, who used them and for what purpose. There are, in the British countryside:

Ridgeways: Probably our oldest tracks, dating back to prehistoric time, old even when our written history began. The Great Ridgeway, winding southern England, and its continuation, the Wessex Ridgeway, are now long-distance paths that you may care to follow. There is the Icknield Way and a number of minor routes. Some of the ridgeways, and other lowland paths, were used as *Herepaths* (paths of the army) by later Saxon armies. Follow them and you could be walking in the steps of Alfred the Great and his Saxon warriors. Along the ridgeway routes lie some of the more important archaeological routes in Britain.

Roman Roads: While many of these have been absorbed into modern trunk roads, there are still a number of stretches marching (not always quite a straight as some would have you believe) across our countryside. Many have become public rights of way. Look for them on the Ordnance Survey maps of your district. The *Ordnance Survey Map of Roman Britain* is a good place to start if you fancy tramping in the steps of the legions.

Holloways: As the name implies these are tracks worn down by the tread of generations of travellers, forming often quite deep hollows in the surrounding land. Sometimes, they may mark some historic boundary, often Saxon.

Pilgrim Routes: Many of the old routes to places of pilgrimage, such as Glastonbury, Walsingham, Glastonbury, Winchester and so on, have been absorbed into modern roads, but there are still stretches worth seeking out. John Adair's book *The Pilgrims' Way* is a good introduction. *Wayfaring Life in the Middle Ages* by J.J. Jusserand is a very good account of how people travelled around England in the late medieval period. One good variation on this would be to walk from one cathedral city to another, on your own personal pilgrimage – there are a number of waymarked routes between some cathedral cities.

Drovers' Roads: Livestock was once moved about Britain on the hoof and many of the wide droving roads they used still exist, particularly in Scotland and the north of England. They often run through very lonely countryside for many miles. To find out more read A.R.B Haldane's *The Drove Roads of Scotland*.

Church Paths: As the name implies these are the local paths used by churchgoers in times past. Some are still used for that purpose today.

Green Lanes: These are really just tracks, hedged on both sides, that were never surfaced and turned into motor lanes. Most are rights of way or accepted access.

Turnpike Roads: Many of these are now part of the modern highways network and not particularly pleasant to walk along. Some old stretches have been bypassed by modern roads and can be used by ramblers. Look out for old milestones, indicating the distance between towns on the route, and former tollhouses and toll gates, where travellers had to pay to use the turnpike. Pedestrians of old used to often walk along roads. Fast and noisy modern traffic is a deterrent in these times.

Coastal Paths: Much of Britain's coastline has a path or paths around it, even if not all of them are rights of way. Some are the tracks used by coastguards as they watched out for smugglers. Many were used by the smugglers themselves! Some have been absorbed into coastal long-distance trails.

Towpaths and Riverside Paths: Alongside rivers or, more usually canals. Most are rights of way or offer public access. Why not walk the canals in the steps of the navigators (navvies) who built them? The books of L.T.C Rolt are worth seeking out if you want to know more about their history. Rivers are well worth following from their source to their mouth (or the other way round). There are often rights of way or at least lanes running parallel to their course. In Scotland, you have a legal right to walk by them in most cases. And it doesn't have to be a mighty river like the Thames or the Severn. There are some delightful rambles alongside some of our tiniest rills.

Robert MacFarlane's recent book The Old Ways *gives an atmospheric account of many of these fascinating old routes. If you wish to preserve these ancient tracks then please support the Ramblers Association and the Open Spaces Society.*

Archaeology: You will get a great deal more out of country walking if you understand something about archaeology. The British landscape is a palimpsest, layers of our history abound. In Norfolk, at Grimes' Graves, you can see where our prehistoric ancestors mined flint. In the Langdale Valley of the Lake District is a prehistoric stone axe factory. Dartmoor has some of the most extensive areas of Bronze Age archaeology in Europe. Britain's high places and downlands offer a close-up look at ancient burial barrows, kistvaens (burial chests), stone rows and circles, solitary standing stones, prehistoric boundaries. Even more recent events such as World War Two offer modern archaeology if you fancy seeking out defensive pill-boxes and coastal defence lines, old wartime airfields. Most counties in Britain have an archaeological society you can join.

Industrial Archaeology: Many parts of Britain have been changed by our industry. Why not walk in the steps of the navvies, the quarrymen, and miners? Old engine houses, mines, tramways and leats can be sought out. There are books on industrial archaeology covering many of our counties. It is worth joining the Association for Industrial Archaeology. Visit their website at www.industrial-archaeology.org

Wild Life: Rambling can easily be combined with watching wildlife, whether it be bird-watching, spotting mammals such as deer and foxes, or studying wild flowers, trees or fungi (Please don't eat the latter unless you an expert – it might kill you!). A pair of binoculars are worth taking and a good field guide. The solitary rambler has the best chance of seeing our native wildlife. It is worth supporting your local wildlife trust, many of which organise wildlife rambles.

Geology: You don't have to be an expert to get a great deal of pleasure from understanding how the land itself was formed. There are many basic guides to geology about. It is worth planning walks around some of the great geological features of Britain, such as the Jurassic Coast in Devon and Dorset, Cheddar Gorge in Somerset, the chalk downlands of Sussex, the Giant's Causeway in Northern Ireland, the eroding coastlines of East Anglia. It is worth carrying a hammer and chisel for samples. This can be combined with collecting fossils, but please be careful if you venture near to crumbling cliffs and quarries.

Churches: Parish churches are a direct link with the past. When we hear church bells pealing out across the countryside, we are hearing the exact sound heard by travellers and those who worked the land over hundreds of years. The history of the countryside and its people is often revealed by the church, which was the focal point of the parish. The rambler will pass a great many during the course of a year's rambles. It is worth getting to know something about church architecture and the history of the church in our landscape. There are a good many written introductions to observing churches written especially for the beginner. *The Observer's Book of Churches*, though out of print, is a fine starting point. Copies can be found in most antiquarian bookshops.

The Rambler's Notebook: It can be very satisfying to keep a notebook detailing each walk you do. Something you can get out and read in years to come, bringing back memories of golden days in our countryside. A small notebook is quite adequate, one that is light to carry in the pocket of your rucksack. Whether you put in a few basic notes or a more detailed account is a matter of personal choice. You might care to start a blog so that other ramblers can share your experiences.

Walking in Literature: Country walking has inspired many of our greatest writers, so why not hunt through the bookshops or library shelves and seek out the writings of those who have gone before? The poet Edward Thomas wrote both prose and poems inspired by his country walks. Try *The Icknield Way*, *The South Country*, and *Collected Poems*. Richard Jefferies wrote a great deal about walking and nature. *Nature Near London*, *The Story of My Heart*, *The Gamekeeper at Home* and *The Amateur Poacher* are good introductions to his work. George Borrow walked and rode over much of Britain. Try *Lavengro*, *The Romany Rye*, *Wild Wales*. William Wordsworth was greatly influenced by his rambles in the Lake District, as was Samuel Taylor Coleridge and Thomas de Quincy. Charles Dickens was a prodigious walker. W.H.Hudson, a great naturalist and walker gave us *Afoot in England* and *A Shepherd's Life*. The list of writings about walking and the countryside is almost.

If you are a fan of English literature why not walk in locations mentioned in novels? Walk the Yorkshire Dales in the steps of the Bronte sisters? Stratford on Avon and the Forest of Arden with a Shakespeare play or his sonnets. Or the Lake District and Norfolk Broads after reading Arthur Ransome's *Swallows and Amazons* novels. Shropshire and several other places in England suggests the *Lone Pine* novels by Malcolm Saville. Walk Wales and Norfolk in the steps of George Borrow, see *Wild Wales* and *Lavengro*. Cumbria against the background of Hugh Walpole's *Herries Chronicles*. Exmoor with R.D. Blackmore's *Lorna Doone*. Dartmoor against the background of Eden Phillpotts' Dartmoor novels. Scotland: Try the novels of Sir Walter Scott, Andrew Greig and Nigel Tranter. A whole series of walks could be inspired by the writings of John Buchan – a great walker himself - not to mention the thirteen-mile

John Buchan Way in the Borders between Peebles and Broughton. Walk Dorset with the novels of Thomas Hardy, J. Meade Faulkner and Geoffrey Household. Cornwall with the novels of Daphne Du Maurier, Sir Arthur Quiller-Couch and Winston Graham. If you want to walk around London find inspiration for those rambles by reading the novels of Charles Dickens and the Sherlock Holmes stories of Sir Arthur Conan Doyle. Ireland with the tales of Walter Macken. These are personal choices and there is no end to this literary rambling!

Chapter Six: Ramblings

To give you a taste of the rambling life, this chapter is devoted to some of my own rambling adventures. Herein, you will find items on rambling philosophy, some adventures in all weathers, thoughts on access to the countryside and trespassing, and descriptions of wild nature. Hopefully, these little pieces might inspire you to go out and explore our beautiful land.

Interlude With Maps

It is doubtful whether the pilgrims of old had much in the way of a map to guide them to the sacred shrines of medieval England, though maps of the country certainly existed by then. Probably written route descriptions sufficed or pilgrim routes were just so well known that there was little doubt about the way. The average Briton rarely travelled from home so there would have been little need for detailed guidance to anywhere. In latter times everyone would have known where the great highways led, aided by the numerous milestones. It was really only in the nineteenth century that the land of Britain became well mapped, and then for the purpose of possible military defence, by the Ordnance Survey – originally a branch of the army.

Today's Britain is one of the best mapped countries in the world and poring over Ordnance Survey maps is a joy unto itself. I have always loved maps, even of places I might never visit. From the contours and shading on what is, after all, a flat piece of paper, I can visualise with some accuracy whole landscapes. But when I actually walk I rarely glance at a map, usually only when I halt, or when I want to identify the name of a hill or farm.

I prefer to navigate from the feel of the countryside around me, spotting the line of an ancient footpath as wends its way across fields, or working out the best way to traverse a mountain ridge from what I see. In this I seem to be different from a lot of ramblers that I know. I have joined them on their walks and noticed that their eyes rarely stray from the map. "The best walk they have ever read" is the phrase that comes to mind

My reluctance to rely on maps, except for points of reference, goes back to childhood explorations of a countryside that I didn't even appreciate *was* mapped. I learned those Staffordshire and Warwickshire acres from memory, progressing a little further each time, until a plan of the entire neighbourhood existed in my mind. I never tried to write it down or draw the salient points, though perhaps I should have done, for this gradual discovery of a land is the method employed by explorers since the world began. It was the way used by Speke and Scott, Amundsen and Burton. We say that people know somewhere "like the back of their hand". That was how I had come to know the country of my childhood, through a constant exposure to its many wonders: from the canal towpath to the ruined farmhouse, from the harvest field to the line of the railway.

Once that landscape was fixed in the memory I could go on to the next portion and the distant land beyond that. It is the way our ancestors must have grasped the 'lie of the land'. Years later I purchased an old map of that corner of Staffordshire and was quietly satisfied at how accurately I had mapped the place in my head.

Exploring without a map can lead to unexpected delights. You get the real thrill of the explorer as you come across the lake you never knew existed, the bluebell wood you never want to leave behind, the old Pele tower guarding a border valley. In later childhood, I explored the immediate countryside around a popular holiday resort, in the way I had roamed the Midlands, not buying a map for several months, but just discovering a mile further each day.

On one occasion, the end of my walk was the brow of a hill. I spotted what looked like a disused road quarry a mile away and decided that it looked sufficiently remote to be the end of the next day's adventuring. Once there I lit a fire and made tea and cooked a meal, the blue wisp of smoke rising into the clear sky. So beautiful and unspoiled did it seem to be that I felt myself in the middle of nowhere. Only afterwards, climbing up past the disused quarry, did I realise that there was a country lane above with occasional passing cars. The feeling of remoteness shrank away for a while, until I discovered the secluded and wooded country beyond.

Sometimes I would make maps of the countryside explored in this way, marking the line of the roads, the green of the woodlands, and the deep valleys. I would give places names that seemed appropriate. Passing a copse I heard a woodsman chopping down a tree, so that became Cutter's Wood. Interestingly, the wood has no name at all on the Ordnance Survey map and a local farmer told me he had forgotten the local name used by his father and grandfather.

I suppose I was influenced a great deal by the children in Arthur Ransome's wonderful series of *Swallows and Amazons* novels, who were forever exploring areas of the Lake District and East Anglia and drawing maps with great proficiency, adding their own names to places. Ransome's books must have influenced a great many British walkers and are as readable today as when they first appeared. Certainly a fair portion of my love of outdoor adventure dates back to my first readings of the Ransome canon.

Whether today's ramblers should even attempt to get to know hill districts without a map is debateable. Even proposing it will probably incur the wrath of mountain rescuers, though I would suggest that very experienced hillwalkers might care to give it a try, perhaps carrying just a compass so that a course might be steered for the nearest road or river if a fog comes down. I see no reason why a stretch of lowland countryside might not be explored in such a way, but even then with great care.

When I came to explore Dartmoor, my first great wilderness area, I certainly had a map, but I still approached my discovery of its acres in much the same way, getting to know a part of the Moor adjacent to a road, then the next mile to, say, a river, then the area next to that. Using this method I soon got to know all of the hills when seen from every possible direction, the course of the streams and the thousands of antiquities left behind from the Bronze Age and the later tin-miners.

My Dartmoor walks led to battles by correspondence with the Ordnance Survey, for some of their early maps showed a number of errors. One was over Cosdon Hill, one of the greatest heights of the northern moor, which bore the prissy name Cawsand on the sheets produced in the nineteen sixties. There was a kind of excuse for this blunder, for local people might pronounce the hill's name as 'Cosson'. But variations of 'Cosdon' were how it appeared in documents dating back to 1240, and that was good enough for me. After a very lengthy exchange of letters the Ordnance Survey conceded the point and today that lovely summit appears on the map as Cosdon Hill.

What was unforgivable was the Ordnance Survey's removal altogether of many local place names, there for all to see on the 1:25000 scale maps in the nineteen fifties, but not on today's much more expensive sheets. Bad enough that the maps have become 'metricated' and that our lovely summits, once measured in thousands of feet, are now in metres, seeming dwarfed in comparison. Despite all of these misgivings maps are lovely creations. One of the great joys in life is to pore over a map as you prepare future expeditions, or recall the exhilarating tramps of yesteryear, or look at places you may never visit.

Walking in Silence

Bertrand Russell once wrote that nobody could have any idea about how quiet the countryside might be unless they had lived and walked before the Great War.

No walk is undertaken in silence. There are always the sounds of the countryside around, the wind soughing through the trees and the birds singing. I like to hear the sound of church bells ringing in the distance, knowing it to be a sound our ancestors would have heard as they looked across the same scene. But the intrusive sounds of the 21st century are a pest, whether they be the distant rumble of traffic or the buzz of aircraft overhead.

I loved that Icelandic volcano of a few years ago! A few magical days of country walking without any aeroplanes overhead. The country poet Edward Thomas before the Great War, referred to an aeroplane overhead – probably the first poetic mention of one of the things. Just reading his poem gives a real feeling of intrusion, a sense that the countryside may never be truly secret again.

Some years ago, I led a trappist walk for my rambling group – a ramble across northern Dartmoor where talking was forbidden, except for a couple of talking breaks. It was an odd experience, particularly when we couldn't say hello to passers-by. But I commend the experiment to you. Best done on open ground where you don't have to see people over lots of stiles or through chatty villages.

And wouldn't it be lovely, never to hear a car engine again? Walking near Cranmere Pool on northern Dartmoor a while ago, I could clearly hear the traffic on the awful Okehampton bypass. A place of solitude defiled. Okay, I'm a motorist too, but it seems to me we have become obsessed with getting to places far too quickly. Cars shouldn't have priority over the peaceful existence of country walkers. They should have to cope with existing roads, with no more dual-carriageways invading our green fields.

And I wish nothing but hell and perdition on the proposed high speed rail link through England that will wrecks dozens of ancient woodlands and carve up hundreds of rights of way. Do we really need a rail line that gets people – almost certainly rich businessmen will be the only people who can afford a ticket – just a bit faster to the north? Wouldn't it be better to invest all that cash on our branch lines, so that the multitude can leave their cars at home and access our beautiful countryside as our forebears did? I don't mind the distant and occasional rumble of a train, particularly if its carriages are carrying real people, not suited idiots who can't see further than their calculators. Nowadays, you have to go further out to avoid the sounds of machinery; far into the Pennines perhaps, or the loneliest glens of Scotland. There you may find just the sounds of nature.

Just occasionally it is possible to hear the quieter sounds of nature without the turgid blare of human interference. But the experience becomes rarer as we progress through this new century. Let us all fight a battle to keep noise and visual intrusion out of our countryside.

Summit Fever

What is it about the summits of mountains and hills? You spend all day getting up to one, perhaps in tearing winds or driving rain, maybe on a still day of heat. Depending on the angle of ascent and distance climbed, you might be breathless and weary. If you are not feeling fit for purpose, you might contemplate giving up, especially when you encounter one false summit after another. But for some reason you rarely do – the summit draws you on. For me the achievement of a summit takes away all of the tiredness and strain. Summits are magical places that instil a new burst of energy and well-being. All of the struggle of the climb vanishes in a moment. It is as though something super-natural occurs, as though you are drawing some *thing* from the place itself, some new strength, some sense of purpose.

And when up on a summit, I find it incredibly difficult to leave, to come down again. It is as though the real world is there on top of that hill or mountain, the place where your soul belongs, far above the delusional, frustrating, annoying, screaming, world below.

On the peak of Cruachan, I found myself in cloud and could barely see a couple of yards. I was in a tiny world of my own, defined by an atmosphere of moving white moisture, womb-like, concentrated. The rest of the universe no longer seemed to matter. Immortal.

Then again on Ben Sgulaird. A beautiful clear June evening, with views right across the Scottish Highlands in one direction and out over Mull and the Hebrides in another. A warm evening, a rich glow over the summer's colouring. All still, hardly a sound but the grazing sheep far below. Peace of mind, only slightly intruded upon by the decision to have to descend.

Searching the mythologies of old, the Greek, the Norse, and so on, is it any wonder past peoples associated mountains with the homes of the gods? For sometimes, summit fever puts you in a godlike state…

Dartmoor Mist

Some of my most memorable walks have been in the mist. There is something quite magical and other-worldly about tramping through wild country when the horizon has closed down to a few yards. For all you can tell, nobody is within miles of you. Standing stones, rocks, fast flowing rivers and antiquities emerge with a suddenness that verges on the miraculous.

Many walkers fear mist and will not venture out in all but the clearest weather. It is true that you lose the view on misty days but, supposing you can use a map and compass with confidence, you make up for that by experiencing our land at its most elemental.

In the consciousness of many who have never visited , somewhere like Dartmoor is a land of mists and mires – literature and popular perception have told them so. Most guide books have at least a few paragraphs expounding the "dangers" of Dartmoor mists, how you might get lost, how you might stumble into a bog or be benighted in the wilderness. This is all true if uncommon. The rambler who claims never to have been mislaid in a mist has never walked very far. If adventure is controlled risk then we should all experience walks in all conditions.

This does depend on the ability to navigate. I am horrified at the number of walkers I encounter who regard the compass around their neck as some kind of talisman, worn for luck and with little idea of how it actually works. Learning to use a map and compass is really easy and opens up the possibility of exploring in all weathers. The weather on places like Dartmoor can change suddenly, plunging the brightest day into gloom, so it is as well to be prepared.

Experience doesn't protect you from the onset of mist. Even the great William Crossing, Dartmoor's greatest interpreter and tramper, got lost upon the Moor. In his book *Amid Devonia's Alps* he recounts a walk to Hexworthy in atrocious weather, not just mist but driving rain, when he got badly lost and only discovered his position by falling into the old mine working at Ringleshutts Girt. In the same chapter he tells how Mrs Hooper, then resident of Nuns Cross Farm, was lost upon the Moor for many hours, going round in circles within a mile of her home.

I have my own experience of being badly lost. As a teenager, walking with a school friend, we got caught by a mist just west of Redlake. We had been properly prepared, but found that our compass had somehow fallen out of our knapsack. We wandered around, and no doubt in circles, for many hours. It was a very thick mist, visibility of no more than a few yards. Obstacles really do become magnified in size when seen in low visibility. Every heather bush on our limited horizon took on the dimensions of a tor until it was actually reached. We found, two or three times, a huge mine gully of a depth that I knew simply didn't exist on southern Dartmoor. I think on reflection it was the one above Hensroost, though the mist gave it massively exaggerated proportions.

We were just considering the possibility of bivvying for the night when my friend (who was training to be a vicar) raised his eyes to heaven and cried out "oh for a sign, a sign". Almost immediately one of the Ter Hill stone crosses loomed out of the mist and the situation was resolved. Even I was a trifle spooked at the coincidence .

Benighted travellers of old supposedly blamed their misfortune on the Dartmoor pixies. To be "pixy-led" means to be led astray. The traditional cure for breaking the spell is to take off your coat and put it on inside out. In his very readable "Hints to the Dartmoor Rambler" at the beginning of his *Guide to Dartmoor*, William Crossing suggests following a river downstream if you are badly lost, which I suppose might be better than dying from exposure. The disadvantages are that you could end up miles from where you want to be and, while you might get away with such a policy on Dartmoor, the same tactic in a mountain district could easily take you over a cliff.

Where Dartmoor is at its most ferocious is when the cloud cover of driving rain – or even snow – brings both mist and wind. This is probably the worst that nature can throw at you, though nightfall compounds the horror. Unless you are an experienced hillwalker it is better not to set out in such conditions and if you get caught up in such conditions to seek shelter as soon as possible.

But what I call the gentle mists of Dartmoor can be a treat, those still days when the mist lingers over valley and hill top. I recall one quiet morning making my way up the Wo Brook is such a mist, the earth still and with no sound of voices to break the peace of the day. It was like being alone in the world, refreshing to the spirit. At the old bridge on the mine track I looked upstream, the few yards I could see, and caught a glimpse of an otter playing, diving into a pool and them repeatedly climbing up on to the bank to do it again and again. After quite a while he headed upstream and vanished into the mist.

It is by such experiences that we discover ourselves, lost or not. The human spirit needs adventure and an element of risk. It is sad that our over-protective society fails to recognise such needs. Dartmoor is just the place for such adventures. Those who know it best know it in all conditions, from bright sunlit summer days to the wilder moments of rough winds and deep mists.

Night Roaming

At night the British countryside takes on a whole new identity, mysterious and forbidding for some, but challenging and exciting for those who dare to cross the threshold and venture outdoors. All through my boyhood I avidly read the tales of old time poaching in the woods of the great estates, of the darkened heaths where highwaymen lurked, and the wild coastlines where smugglers landed their cargoes after midnight.

There is a long tradition of more innocent night roaming, from the naturalist in search of our more elusive wildlife to the literary man in search of inspiration. Charles Dickens is a good example of the latter, an insomniac wandering the streets of London from dusk until dawn and the country lanes around Gads Hill, composing his stories in his head as he went.

On moonlit nights I often used to meander on Dartmoor, across a landscape that seemed unearthly, something far apart from the workaday world of the Devon towns. Nightwalking the Moor has enjoyed something of a popularity in recent years, useful as a way of teaching navigation across wild countryside. And this is not just an activity for the military. The Dartmoor explorer Ted Birkett Dixon became renowned for his group walks at night in the last years of the old century, finding many willing volunteers. I used to lead group walks on Dartmoor at night in the 1970s, though I found more enjoyment by walking alone.

Now some people will argue that a rocky and boggy place like Dartmoor is difficult enough to negotiate in broad daylight. I am often asked whether I can see anything at all, or whether I am walking in total blackness. But night roaming is not walking blind. The truth is that there is a great deal of light in the countryside, particularly when the moon is full. The secret is to let your eyes become adapted to what light there is, and to resist the temptation to use a torch which can ruin your night vision for many minutes. I recall on one expedition where I had walked in darkness from Merivale to North Hessary Tor and was able to see far out across the moorland, so good had my night vision become. But once across the tor I came into full view of Dartmoor Prison and was dazzled by its intensive security lights and seemed almost blinded for a good half hour. I staggered back with quite a lot of difficulty.

My favourite night walk on Dartmoor, the one that comes to mind whenever I recall those youthful nights of exploration, is one across the higher summits of the south Moor. From Bittaford I walked into the wild, climbing Western Beacon and then following the ridge to Three Barrows. It was a warm still night, not a breeze, the only sound my feet crunching on the moor grass, for there had been weeks without rain. Once into the Moor, the lights of the villages and traffic faded away, though on the hilltops were the lights and glow of the city of Plymouth and, now and again, the flashes from lighthouses. It was a good clear night of stars, for the moon was not yet risen. There were the famous constellations, seeming so large that it felt as though you might reach up and touch them. I lay on my back beside one of the stone cairns on Three Barrows and watched the bright light of a satellite pass overhead.

I wandered up to Redlake and sat beside the waste tip of the old time china clay quarries. These days it has grassed over, but then it was shining white and luminous as it caught the first light of the rising moon, the great pond beneath turning from blackness to gold as I watched. I threw in a stone and watched the reflection of the moon quiver. A vixen yelped nearby, and the sheep stirred. Not a human soul seemed to be on the Moor that night, the hut circles, warreners' huts, and stone rows left to their memories and their ghosts. As the sheep settled the space around returned to an unearthly quiet, the only sounds coming when I moved on, from my footsteps on the heather. As I absorbed the solitude of the Moor and found an ease within it I thought that there was no better place to be on that summer's night.

Somewhere on the long slopes of Ryder's Hill I found a badger sett. Now people think of badgers as creatures of woodland, but they have a great many homes on the open hillsides of Dartmoor. This sett was like a great earthen fortress, surrounded by bracken, flattened where the brocks had rolled it down, permeated by a dozen paths by which the animals made their way down to the river. Badgers tend to leave these open setts much later in the night than they might do if they were surrounded by woodland. The badgers had been long out by the time I discovered their home, but I was fortunate to see two returning from their nightly perambulations, grunting with impatience as they both tried to enter the same hole at the same time, their noise echoing from one side of the valley to the other. Drenched in moonlight I arrived on the summit of Ryder, all the moorland world around yellow in the glow. Distant lights showed where there might be people, but no one was in sight. I felt like the last man on earth as I looked back into the darkness of the moorland miles I had traversed.

The Nine Standards

I have always liked the little town of Kirkby Stephen, an unpretentious halting point on the Coast to Coast from St Bees Head to Robin Hood's Bay, a tremendous long distance walk devised by the greatest of all fellwalkers, Alfred Wainwright. The town itself is without airs, a long street leading to an old market square where goods have been sold since its market charter was granted in 1361. Its large church is even older, boasting some wonderful ancient tombs, and displaying a carved cross, sacred to the Norse god Loki, which is well over a thousand years old.

The centre of Kirkby Stephen is a busy place, filled with people coming and going; with farmers shopping and ramblers following in Wainwright's footsteps. There is a friendliness about the people in these parts; they stop for a chat, and serve you with a smile in the local shops.

I saw the Nine Standards at a distance on my first visit to Kirkby Stephen, strange standing objects on the long Pennine ridge, several miles out of the town. I didn't know what they were but soon found out. Nine Standards Rigg, the Ordnance Survey map calls them. Tall cairns atop the hill, like old grey men keeping a weary watch. One of the legends about the Nine Standards is that they were built to convince raiding Scots that a deterring army was encamped upon the hill. A simpler explanation is that the Nine Standards are boundary stones. Whatever the reason for their construction, they are massive and can be seen from miles away in all directions.

On a beautifully clear April morning I sat on a bench close by Frank's Bridge, below the town, preparing to walk up the long hill to the Nine Standards. The very narrow Frank's Bridge crosses the River Eden on the line of an ancient lich way into the town, the route by which corpses were transported to the church in Kirkby Stephen. Now it seems to be where the residents of the town come to relax, to sit by the river and feed the ducks. It is certainly a very pleasant place to linger, and it took some effort to tear myself away and head for the hills, or more immediately the attractive village of Hartley, a mile away from the town.

I followed Fell Lane as it curved round a massive and unsightly aggregates quarry and headed steeply uphill to become a charming and unfenced country lane. In the distance stretched the snow-covered summit of Wild Boar Fell, where Sir Richard Musgrave supposedly slaughtered the last wild boar in these parts. There may be some truth in this legend, for when his tomb in Kirkby Stephen church was opened in the nineteenth century two tusks were found with his body. They may be seen in a small exhibition case in that building to this day.

Fell Lane petered out on the north west edge of Hartley Fell, becoming a rough track. Every now and again I would get glimpses of the Nine Standards, sometimes seeming to be very near and then farther away, in the usual habit of summits, where you feel that you are about to arrive, only to be surprised by another climbing mile. At one point a couple of guiding cairns by the side of the track created the optical illusion of *being* the Standards, only to thwart me as I came abreast of them. I was on the open fell side by now, heading directly towards the Nine Standards by the side of a tumbling beck called Faraday Gill.

The first real sight of the Nine Standards makes the long uphill from Kirkby Stephen well worthwhile. The cairns are magnificent, huge stone giants strung almost in a line along the hillside. There is something almost forbidding about their presence which dominates the edge of such lonely moorland. As I wandered there, I considered why they were built. I can well believe that this spectacle might deter some passing invader; the cairns have that air about them.

I do not accept the theory that they were erected as boundary stones. Why build so many? And the boundary of what? No one has ever dated the Nine Standards. They could be prehistoric, but are probably of much later date. Whatever, they are bold and mysterious, standing like old grey men on the border between the cultivated valley of the Eden and the remote stretches of this northern wilderness.

One point is not in dispute. The Nine Standards can be seen for miles around, and the view from them takes your breath away. To the highest Pennine height of Cross Fell to the north, and across to the Lakeland fells and the dales of Yorkshire. As I walked around the moorland, grouse took to the sky, muttering cries of annoyance, and skylarks, hardly visible, hovered and sung.

It is hard to grasp the scale of this great wilderness, one of the remotest areas of Britain. There is such a feeling of space amidst such moorland, a rarity in our overcrowded island. I felt high, and had a wonderful energy, as though I were breathing extra oxygen.

Nine Standards Rigg is a hard place to leave behind, and I reluctantly turned downhill to Kirkby Stephen. As I descended my mind drifted into the old times of this place, when fire and blood were the indicators of conflict in this remote region. I looked across the valley beyond the little town of Brough to Stainmore, where the Viking king Eric Bloodaxe was ambushed and slain. There were terrible times in this now peaceful landscape. Perhaps the old stone men of Nine Standards mark the site of some long-forgotten battle?

They are certainly a symbol of these very wild Pennines.

A Morning on Silver How

The other day, we spent a pleasant morning walking up Silver How from Grasmere. I'm with Wainwright when he says "a lovely name for a lovely fell". And it is always good to be in Grasmere itself, cradled amongst those mountains in a quite beautiful setting. Ignore the crowds and spend a while in Sam Read's legendary bookshop, or that antique place along the road that sells such a goodly selection of second-hand and antiquarian Lakeland books.

Silver How has always been a favourite of mine, for the views all around are quite superb, not only across Grasmere and Rydal Water, but of the great circuit of the Fairfield Horseshoe, over Helm Crag towards Blencathra, towards the Langdale Pikes and Wetherlam. And then the great silver length of distant Windermere and a tiny glimpse of Coniston Water.

We did the classic ascent via Wordworth's former home at Allen Bank (which the National Trust have at last opened to the public) and Wray Gill. Just saw a pair of antlers above the bracken but only a very quick view of the deer. It is a lovely fell walk, each turn of the track opening up new and exciting views.

If it didn't have such a beautiful name already, you could rename Silver How "Juniper Mountain" for there is lots of Juniper on its slopes, very prominent as you cross by the tiny waterfalls of the Wray Gill. Then across open ground to the summit with that grand view. A good place to linger on fine days, though I have crouched against driving wind and rain in the past. We were lucky. Dry and clear.

In the past I have used this climb as a starting point for longer fell walks – to Loughrigg, to Blea Rigg and into Easedale, very pleasant rambles which can then be extended again, depending on fitness and mood. But I have always enjoyed Silver How for its own sake, descending in the direction of Loughrigg, before turning under its Grasmere face and down the path to the start of the Red Bank road, not far out of the village, which is what we did the other day. If you are looking for your first Lake District mountain to climb, then Silver How might be a good place to start and get a feel for the place.

A Rainy Walk in Eden

Like the poet Edward Thomas, I can find considerable pleasure in walking in the rain, whether in the mountains or across lowland pastures. On a very wet spring day I arrived in Appleby to explore the lovely countryside by the River Eden. Appleby is best known as the setting for a famous horse fair, when Gypsies and travellers arrive from all over Britain to buy and sell horses, tell fortunes, and snatch a few moments of a journeying way of life that is now no more. There were no Gypsies in sight as I wandered up the main street towards the castle, under threatening skies.

Appleby was once the county town of Westmorland, until sad and unimaginative bureaucrats erased that ancient county from the map. Not that you would know that on the ground, for the spirited folk of the district have maintained their "Welcome to Westmorland" signs at the old county boundaries, and few ever talk of Appleby being in Cumbria.

To keep its old county town traditions alive, the town of Appleby changed its name to Appleby in Westmorland. Westmorland is surely one of the most beautiful words in our language. Let us hope it is not too long before the hideous catch-all of Cumbria is despatched into obscurity, and these wild regions restored to the old counties of Westmorland, Cumberland and Lancashire.

Appleby's castle has been shut to the public for a number of years because of some squabble between its owners and English Heritage – a pity, because its buildings are a fine sight, high above the River Eden. As I looked at it through the castle gate the rain began to speckle down, and by the time I was on the banks of the Eden it was pouring, bouncing and dancing on the surface of the river.

Walking the meadows by the Eden is very pleasant, even in wet weather. The right of way is a real poachers' path, sometimes running across open fields, then through the woodlands that edge down to the course of the river. The pastures were crammed with sheep, the ewes moving their many lambs uphill and out of my range before following me from stile to stile, making a terrific noise as they went. I posited the idea that they had been trained thus by the local river board to draw attention to illicit fishermen. Only in the woods would any poacher be free from observation.

By now the rain was pelting down, and I sought shelter in a walking cape. My walking cape is almost a portable tent that pulls over my entire body, head, rucksack and all, leaving exposed just the lower half of the legs. It can only be used on lowland walks as it catches the wind too much on higher ground. The cape is very effective; you really feel that you are shut off from the worst elements of the weather.

I loathe waterproofs generally, finding them clammy and, after a while, ineffective. There have been days when I have been thoroughly soaked thanks to a reluctance to wear one of the wretched things. But on days of persistent rain I usually start with one on. Yet despite the weather I felt free and happy and considered that every day not spent afoot was a day wasted. I sheltered for a moment or two under a railway viaduct of the Settle to Carlisle line, and then walked into the tiny village of Great Ormside.

The old church is mostly Norman, but built high on a defensive mound which started out as a pagan burial ground. It was here that the Ormside Bowl was found in 1823, probably a Saxon relic looted by the Viking inhabitants of this place.

Standing by the church door I could imagine how the people of Ormside might seek refuge in the church during troublous times. The old building could well survive a short siege and, with the nearby Pele Tower, might deter Scottish warriors who would seek easier prey. It was on an expedition to quell the might of Scotland that the Black Prince, that martial son and heir to Edward III, passed this way in 1376. Feeling unwell he made his will at Great Ormside, courtesy of the church's priest John de Grote. He died soon afterwards, before completing his journey north. Such are the ways that the greater history of England touches the most seemingly forgotten places.

Certainly, the world seems to have passed by Great Ormside. The public house seemed to be shut up as I walked up the village street, but a Gypsy wagon added colour to the scene. Railway trains run by the village, but the station is now a private home. There seemed to be no one about so I walked out of the village to an isolated cottage with the intriguing name of 'Donkey's Nest' called more prosaically 'Porch Cottage' on the Ordnance Survey map, from which a muddy footpath took me over to Rutter Force.

There are some places in Britain that picture postcards might have been invented for, and the waterfall of Rutter Force is one, with its accompanying mill building and waterwheel, a couple of attractive cottages, a ford, and a rustic bridge. I had seen it before in pictures. Indeed, every shop in the district sells pictures, cards and prints of this idyllic scene. Even in the pouring rain it looked pretty, and I leaned against the bridge and admired its crashing waters for several minutes.

I had left the Eden by now, for Rutter Force is on its tributary the Hoff Beck, a charming little river where the water runs light over rocky shillets before plunging into deep pools. On one stretch of water I encountered a flotilla of some forty ducklings, swimming in tight formation from bank to bank, until scattered by a pair of herons coming in to land.

The little hamlet of Hoff consists of a pub and a few cottages, but it marks a wilder stretch of the Hoff Beck, its bank lined with stretches of heath and woodland. There must be a tale attached to one wooded bend of the beck called Cuddling Hole, but if there is, I have been unable to discover it. Its proximity to the back of Appleby, not to mention the deep riparian cover, would make it an admirable venue for courting couples. Probably not in the rain, though.

But if I did not discover any concealed lovers, I did find traces of what I am sure must have been an old drove road, descending both banks to a crossing point over the water. You come across such remnants of the droving trade all over the north of England and the Scottish Borders. Happy is the walker who has the opportunity to devote time to their exploration, I considered as I sat on the slope above the little footway of Bandley Bridge sipping tea, and staring out from my hood at the still pouring rain. But all the birds of spring were still singing in this very peaceful countryside.

It was just a stroll back into Appleby from Bandley Bridge, the rain easing a little as it tends to do just as you are finishing a walk. But some months later I did again the walk to Rutter Force and the Hoff Beck, this time in the baking heat of one of the hottest summers on record.

As I ascended the hill from Bandley Bridge I came upon the local farmer and his wife gathering in the harvest from the great field atop the ridge, their harvesters laying out great rolls of hay, for all the world like chickens laying eggs. Some way up the field were the farming couple by their landrover. We talked, as farmers and walkers so often do when they come together, of the weather, the great blaze of sun and drought that had beset the land for months.

I told them of my walk in the rain, not so long before, as we all eyed a sky of unbroken blue. They took a great interest in where I had been, such are the friendly folk of Westmorland, a reminder that there does not always have to be conflict between walkers and understanding landowners. Sitting in a café in Appleby I reflected on this walk under the brow of the high Pennines, and made notes on my wet day in Eden, the beautiful little church at Great Ormside and the quiet pastures around the Hoff Beck.

Sometimes, in reflective mood, I sit at home and look back on these walks and find it hard to believe that there are such places in what so often seems overcrowded England. As I sipped my cup of tea that day in Appleby, a horse drawn Romany wagon crossed the old bridge and took the road leading to the wilder country of the north Pennines, a sight that gladdened my heart, being so far removed from the terrors of twenty-first century life and all that makes the modern world something that you wish to escape from. I picked up my rucksack and headed once more to the outdoors.

Walking to High Cup Nick

High Cup Nick is a symbol of the wild and untamed nature of the northern hills, a massive gash that makes any wandering humans seem irrelevant in scale. This incredible place is very familiar to anyone who has walked the higher stretches of the Pennine Way, for the oldest of our National Trails turns westward by the Nick and makes the long descent to the village of Dufton. To approach High Cup Nick in such a way, after miles of moorland walking, must be quite an experience, like tumbling off the edge of the world.

There was still snow on the Pennines highest summit, Cross Fell, as I walked out from Dufton in a circuitous route that would take me to High Cup Nick from the south.

Charming was the woodland scenery of Dufton Gill Wood, its St Bees sandstone rocks exposed for all too see in this landscape of wild and very visible geology. As I walked across farmland to Keisley Bridge, I remained on low ground, the great ridge of the Pennines to the east. This is the land of the Helm, that great stormy wind that can sweep without mercy down into the vale from the neighbouring hills.

I sat for a while on the parapet of the bridge over the Keisley Beck. This was what the roaming life was really all about. Just one individual in the heart of wild nature. My heart was merry, and I could have danced over the stile before me. It was a weekday and this was a holiday. I considered the millions in work that very same day, perhaps doing jobs that were an anathema to them, maybe for poor pay. I have done such work myself, dreading the lightening of the morning when I had to set out for another day's wage slavery. Whereas I had the freedom of the hills to look forward to, the hours were my own and I could go wherever I wanted to. Shackles loosened, I made my way passed a farm with the odd name of Harbour Flatt and then out on to the open fells.

This is wonderfully untamed country, where the Pennines drop so suddenly to the flood plains of the River Eden. Such a contrast of lands too, the wild moorland set against the flatter lands of wood and meadow. The track I followed led out on to the slopes of a very rocky hill called Middletongue, high above the tumbling waters of Trundale Gill, itself in as spectacular valley as any fellwalker might wish for.

As I climbed higher and higher, I found myself in the midst of wild and exposed moorland, broken up with patches of whin sill rock and hundreds of shake holes, a land shattered by the forces of geology. As I paused I could see the cultivated fields of Eden spread out from horizon to horizon, north to south, whilst before me were mile after mile of lonely fell. Skylarks hovered and danced overhead, and everywhere were the mournful cries of curlew and snipe.

I took my own line over Middletongue to the southern rim of High Cup Nick, where I stood in silence, bewildered by the incredible sight before me. Descriptions and photographs do not do justice to High Cup Nick. In all my long years of walking I had never seen anything quite like it. This great gash in the Pennines almost defines the words, awesome, forbidding, magnificent. It is a deep canyon, boxed with mighty cliffs at one end, bar a narrow cut where the waters of High Cupgill Beck tumble through and down, the wind from the west blowing its spray back over the lip of the fall towards the moorland above. An overhanging lip of whin sill lines the edges of the great valley, huge slopes of grey scree climbing up to meet it, these cliffs broken by the white lines of waterfalls, tiny becks achieving majesty as they tumble hundreds of feet to join the river far below.

High Cup Nick seemed like one of those places in legend where quests are resolved, where heroes engage in final battles, and where the mighty come to die.

I wandered around the southern rim to the waterfall itself, finding quite a tiny beck flowing in from the gentle slope of the fells. I scrambled a little way down the waterfall to get the best view down the valley, the westerly wind blowing the odd spume across my back, cooling in the hot weather. The thought occurred to me that this must be a terrible place when the Helm Wind is at its fiercest.

I followed the route of the Pennine Way around the Nick's northern edge and clambered out on to the rocky crag known as Nichol's Chair, supposedly named after a Dufton cobbler who sat there and mended some shoes. It was a precarious perch for me just sitting still, the great drop below reminding me that I was not immortal. But it was a wonderful place to be, and I was filled with the sheer joy of living. I remembered the schoolteacher who branded me 'challenge dependent' at quite an early age.

Perhaps he was right.

I pulled back a short distance to eat lunch on the edge of the Pennine Way, waving a greeting at a party of quite elderly ramblers who came by, heading for the head of the waterfall. I watched as they reached there and then they disappeared down into the chasm. I thought that they had probably just halted for lunch, but the sounds of exhilarated yelling from the party took me back to the edge. There they were, scrambling down the boulder field beside the waterfall and evidently enjoying every minute of the experience. Now I had glimpsed them on the way up the track and the youngest must have been way over seventy. I watched as they reached the bottom of the cliff, and smiled at their great shouts of triumph.

I headed down the Pennine Way back to Dufton, stopping every few yards to gain yet a different view of High Cup Nick and, in the other direction, a vista of the familiar mountains of the Lake District. As I turned a corner in the track, High Cup Nick was lost from view, and I plodded into Dufton, where I sat for a while on the green, reminiscing about the day's walk. I like Dufton, the village of the doves, its cottages lining a pleasant green, with the fells still in sight. W.H. Auden thought it the prettiest village in England.

A few days later, I was in Bowness-on-Windermere and strolled into a place selling antiquarian books and prints, for old books about the countryside are a passion for me. There was nothing I wanted in the book line, but among the framed prints I found an old engraving of High Cup Nick. It adorns my wall to this day and I cannot pass it without recalling the moody atmosphere of that great cleft in the western edge of the Pennines.

Under the Helm Wind: *The Pennines north of the Eden is the land of the Helm, that great stormy wind that can sweep without mercy down into the vale from the neighbouring hill. Its very name coming from the Vikings who early settled this area. I have not yet witnessed it, but it is reported to be one of those terrible manifestations of nature that are never forgotten, once experienced. William*

Wordsworth's friend Thomas Wilkinson described it thus, in his 1824 book *Tours to the British Mountains:*

"An assemblage of pale clouds extends to the summit of the mountain (Cross Fell); and, when all is calm on the plains, a roaring like the sea is heard to a considerable distance. I was once involved in the Helm Winds:- if I advanced it was with my head inclined to the ground, and at a slow pace; if I retreated and leaned against it with all my might, I could hardly keep erect; if I did not resist it I was blown over. A wind from the east rushed down the mountain with incredible fury: it broke the boughs from the trees, and tore the thatch from cottages at Melmerby and Gamblesby. But when I left this elemental tumult about two miles, all was perfectly calm, and a little further a gentle breeze sprang up from the West, while behind me the Helm Winds continued raging with unabated fury. Having heard uproars among mankind, and uproars among the elements, I prefer the latter, as having more sublimity."

Circling Dufton Pike

As you drive along the A66 from Penrith to Appleby, the great western edge of the Pennines looms across the Eden valley. On the edge of this mighty range of hills are three distinct pikes, Knock Pike, Dufton Pike and Murton Pike– all worthy of a climb. But the paths around the pikes are well worth a walk too, offering a variety of excellent shorter walks.

We set off from Dufton to circle Dufton Pike. The first part of the ramble, up Hurning Lane, is part of the Pennine Way. The lane is an old green track, with attractive stone clam bridges, and rough rock paving slabs alongside the wet bits. After an initial shower, the weather cleared to a beautiful day of bright blue skies, offering distant views of snow-covered fells around Shap and the eastern Lake District.

As we climbed Cosca Hill, the Pennine Way became exceptionally muddy, but then there has been a great deal of rain and melting snow. Walking above the track made the going a lot easier. We left the Pennine Way at the Great Rundale Beck, to walk the far side of Dufton Pike. A lovely grassy track winds high above the beck, through a quiet lost valley where time seems to have stood still, a sanctuary from our hurried modern world, offering views up to the Whin Sill of Threlkeld Side, a magnificent canyon, a smaller version of the more famous High Cup Nick.

As we turned the corner of the Pike and descended back to Dufton, much of the Eden valley, distant Pennine heights and the Howgills came into view, some of the higher ground covered in snow, ending a grand walk in really good weather. It has been said, rightly, that if the Lake District didn't exist, this part of Cumbria would be thronged with fellwalkers. As it happened we saw only a distant shepherd with his dog. These really are grand and somewhat neglected hills.

A Ramble From Cartmel.

Not all interesting Cumbrian walks have to be on the high fells, even though the best usually are. There are many quiet and scenic rights of way in the Cartmel area. From the racecourse I walked out into wilder pastoral country and stretches of woodland, to a beautiful stream with a ford and old stone clam bridge. One of those quiet places that time seems to have missed, but possibly the way William de Walton walked, when he was the prior of Cartmel in the 13th Century. His residence, Walton Hall, is now just a farm, and my path took me through its yard.

Beyond Hill Farm is lovely unspoiled country, though at one point I struggled to find a path that no longer seems to exist. But back on a bridleway that definitely does I was soon out into a landscape of turf, bracken and trees, where the humble bees hummed on thistles and the air was full of birdsong. Beautifully peaceful this stretch, with little evidence of the hand of man, bar the stone walls.

On then to Wall Nook Farm. It was here that Arthur Ransome, author of *Swallows and Amazons*, spent three idyllic summers before the Great War, writing his earliest books, going for long walks and learning how to wrestle. Just beyond I crossed an old stone stile and made my way through several fields, before finding myself at Well Knowe, home of Ransome's poet friend Gordon Bottomley. Here Ransome's friend, the poet and essayist Edward Thomas stayed, acquiring the cutting of Old Man which he planted on at several of his homes in Hampshire.

This is a peaceful landscape, broken only by the sound of the farmer calling in his cattle for milking. Above the racecourse, the path wound through woodland, before descending to the racecourse itself (the route across the course needs to be better waymarked). Good, though, these walks, with literary links. Did Edward Thomas think of his days in this quiet place in the horrendous days in the trenches, before his death at the Battle of Arras at Easter 1917?

Walking High Tove and High Seat

Wainwright is unenthusiastic about these two Lake District fells. He didn't like bogs very much. Mind you, these are very mild bogs compared with, say, Dartmoor, where you can get in up to your chest. The bogs around High Tove and High Seat are really just badly drained ground, annoying and tiring but not particularly deep. I imagine that Wainwright baggers just sigh, carry on, and dream of loftier, better-drained fells.

We walked up from Watendlath, on a sweltering day with scarce a relieving breeze, across the broken ground, wet sponges and peat hags, first to High Tove, a modest cairn on a high point of moorland, and then along – well, I was going to say a ridge, but it isn't in any accepted sense of the word, more a heathery swelling – to the rockier and much better looking High Seat. The walking was hard work, the heat beating down, a far tougher proposition than the modest mileage would suggest.

Why bother? Well, for the views. In one direction Gable and Scafell, another the Helvellyn Range, to the north the great peaks of Skiddaw and Blencathra. Worth all the slog for that, for as all-round viewpoints they are superb. Afterwards, we took a very original and probably unwise line of descent via the slopes above Reecastle Crag and Goat Crags and then a diversion around Raise Gill, all of this only recommended if you have bags of energy and don't mind rough heather walking, climbing fences and bog-trotting. Thank God for the Watendlath Tea Garden where they serve the tea in huge mugs. We needed tea on intravenous drip!

Loughrigg Terrace and the Rydal Corpse Road

After weeks of rain the weather relented to give us a fine summer day in the Lakes. Leaving Rydal church we walked down to the River Rothay, climbing up to the great cave at Loughrigg quarries, the remnants of a once-busy slate industry – a massive cave. Wainwright says in his *Central Fells* guide that you could get the population of Ambleside within – I suspect you can, though, as the great man said, some would be standing in water. It was wetter yesterday, after all the rain, than I have ever seen it. Its waters clear, Rydal looked delightful in the sunshine, a heron flapped down beside us, perhaps a descendant of herons known to William and Dorothy Wordsworth.

This route is my favoured climb up to the summit of Loughrigg Fell, that modest height that offers such wonderful views in all directions, particularly up to the mountains of the Fairfield Horseshoe. But, after a bit of a lay-off, we fancied an easy walk, so followed the path on to Loughrigg Terrace. A very clear day, as we looked at the views over Grasmere to Dunmail Raise. Then down through the woods at Red Bank and into the village. We walked out then to Dove Cottage, then up to White Moss Tarn, where Wordsworth used to ice-skate, then on the coffin route back to Rydal.

I like following corpse roads, those ways used by our ancestors to convey the departed to their final burial. You really feel that you are walking in the steps of history on these old paths. *Another reason why ramblers should resist most path diversions.* I have followed a number of Lych Ways around the country, from the famous one across the wilds of Dartmoor to more modest routes in East Anglia. They are worth seeking out. Walking them is a fascinating hobby.

From a scenic point of view the Rydal coffin route is one of the best in the country, with some excellent examples of coffin stones, places where the dead might be rested – to the relief of the carriers. In earlier times, there would have been no coffins, just a shroud of wool. For a long time using a woollen shroud was compulsory, a way of boosting the economy and keeping England's wool industry going.

This coffin route runs from Ambleside to Grasmere Church, and most of it can still be followed away from present-day roads. We were walking it backwards in effect, only doing the stretch from Grasmere to Rydal. Its original beginnings, from Ambleside to Rydal, provides a good route for you between the two points of the Fairfield Horseshoe.

Walking into Borrowdale

Borrowdale from the Watendlath Bridleway. One of the most perfect days of the year, weather wise. One of those Lake District days you dream about, dry, warm, clear views over miles of mountain and fell. All too rare, particularly during very wet summers. But we had one on the day we set out from Watendlath to walk into Borrowdale, taking the bridleway above Bowdergate Gill down by Birkett's Leap and into Borrowdale to Rosthwaite. And what a view! In the clear air every rock and bracken stalk for miles clearly delineated, far distant views to the mountain ranges around Fleetwith Pike and Great Gable.

Crossing the little bridge over Stonethwaite Beck we crossed the Borrowdale Road into Rosthwaite. We had started early and seen but a handful of fellwalkers on the higher ground, but Rosthwaite was busy with ramblers setting out for the day's walk. We headed down to the Derwent and followed that lovely river downstream below Castle Crag and Millican Dalton's Cave. The woods were idyllic, offering some shade from an increasingly hot sun, as we walked towards Grange. In the quieter stretches of river people bathed, canoed and rafted.

The path across the boardwalks at around the head of Derwent Water offered wonderful views across the lake towards Keswick and Skiddaw. There were climbers ahead on Shepherd's Crag. The distant shouts reminding me of rock-climbing days in my youth.

From High Lodore we climbed the steep wooded escarpment, crossing the Watendlath Beck by wading and following it upstream to its little bridge. Then up the permissive path back to Watendlath, buzzards mewing in the mighty Reecastle Crags.

A Wet Walk on Loughrigg Fell

In height, Loughrigg is one of Lakeland's more modest fells, but as an all round viewpoint it is excellent. It is a superb fell walk even on the wettest of days. I walked it in driving rain from Grasmere by way of Dale Head and Red Bank. Heading up the lane the rain seemed to be coming at me from every angle, turning every gap in the stone walls into fierce little waterfalls, battering at the clumps of foxgloves on the hedgebanks. Then out on to the open fell, across the end of Loughrigg Terrace and up the steep path to the top of the fell.

Looking back through the rain, low clouds swept over the waters of Grasmere, the wind buffeting the occasional small rowing boat. But as I climbed higher the clouds hid any view, the rain and wind sweeping the hill. There was no one else on Loughrigg that I saw and for once I had its summit all to myself, though I could see but a few yards.

The weather was too wild too linger, so I walked down the path to Chapel Stile for a while, reluctant to leave Loughrigg's higher ground. I wandered up and down for an hour, and in that time the rain swept away and the wind suddenly died. The sun made a tentative appearance. Soon there were views all around and a bright sun dispelled the mist.

I descended the way I had come for the views over Grasmere and all its friendly and familiar surrounding fells. Grasmere's waters had calmed. Two men were fishing on the banks below the terrace. Canada Geese were feeding in the wet fields on the edge of the mere. A good walk and the sheer joy of being back in the Lakes. Then tea in Grasmere and a browse in Sam Read's bookshop. Walking and a bookshop – two of the joyous hallmarks of English civilisation.

Walking on Easdon

I would put money on the fact that the top of the great hill of Easdon is Dartmoor's least visited summit. Understandable. It is not on the way to anywhere and cannot be easily linked with any neighbouring hill tops. Walking the top from Manaton or North Bovey is a very short and easy ascent, just a few miles, some of the journey along lanes and bridleways.

So why do it? Easy answer. Easdon is one of the best all round viewpoints on Dartmoor, giving the hillwalker a wide vista of the Moor from Cosdon to Rippon Tor in one direction and the Dartmoor borderlands, Great Haldon and the heathlands of east Devon in the other.

The summit rocks of Easdon. This great round hill, rising like a resting volcano above the tiny medieval fields of the River Bovey valley. I hadn't been on the hill for several years. There had been refreshing rain in the night and the countryside felt fresh as we set out in bright sunshine. We did the walk from Manaton, where hidden bees buzzed furiously in the lime trees surrounding the village green. We walked through the churchyard, past the old stone cross – which a previous vicar once buried to stop his pagan parishioners from dancing around it.

Okay, the first part of the walk is not the most exciting mile on Dartmoor. Along the lane for much of the way, with just one footpath to cut a corner. But there wasn't much traffic about and the views of Hayne Down, with its mighty rock pile of Bowerman's Nose are grand. Then up the quiet lane by Barracott Farm, that ascends into a green lane and bridleway.

Out on the open moorland of Easdon at last and following the old stone wall round to the great rock pile of Figgy Daniel or Dan'l, as the locals say. Like the greater hill on which it is situated, Figgy Dan'l seldom gets visitors. And that is a pity, for it is as good a Dartmoor tor as many better known ones. It offers better views over eastern Dartmoor than many more frequented places. As a climbing rock, Dan'l is easier to ascend than the better known Bowerman's Nose. And it is just ten minutes easy walking from the summit of Easdon.

Now I have walked Easdon is all sorts of weather, in the thickest of fogs and wildest hours of wind and rain. I have sunbathed on its top on summer afternoons and watched the cloud shadows chasing across its neighbouring hills. But this climb was probably the best of all those days for visibility. The light was perfect, every Dartmoor tor, hillside and piece of rock sharply drawn. As always, when a summit has been attained, there was a great reluctance to head downhill.

It has to be said the northern slopes of Easdon have become infested with bracken. The track down to the Luckdon bridleway is clear enough at first, but is soon swamped by this perfidious fern. It is such a pity, for much of the Bronze Age archaeology that proved so fascinating to earlier visitors is now concealed. Disastrously, the rhizomes of the bracken are almost certainly damaging the buried archaeology. Easdon is a very contained hill, surrounded by the fields and woods of the in-country. It should not be too difficult for the Dartmoor National Park Authority, or the Dartmoor Preservation Association, with its much-vaunted bracken-bashing programme, to declare war on Easdon's bracken.

From Luckdon, we followed the lane and footpaths to Manaton Rocks, through stretches of oakwood where the very roots of the trees have become entangled with huge boulders, like the setting for stories by the Brothers Grimm or Tolkien.

I well remember Manaton Rocks before the public footpath was fenced, implying that ramblers may not wander freely around these this lovely tor. Many years ago, Devon Ramblers and the Dartmoor Preservation Association opposed the fencing. I took part in that battle myself. But the National Park Authority, which sides too often with landowning interests, let the fencing pass. They assured Dartmoor walkers that it would be temporary. Decades later it is still there, a monstrous intrusion in this beautiful place. Surely, time for it to go? And why wasn't Manaton Rocks mapped as access land under CRoW (Countryside and Rights of Way Act). If this isn't open country then what is?

But despite problems with bracken and fencing there is much beautiful countryside to be seen by walking Easdon and Manaton Rocks. This quieter area of Dartmoor deserves to be better known.

In Search of Pixies Holt

In my talks with Dartmoor walkers I am always surprised at how few have ever been to Pixies Holt. Many confuse it with the education adventure centre on the hill out of Dartmeet, which bears the same name and in truth the legendary lair of the little folk of Dartmoor is not very far away. I suspect that one difficulty is finding the cave in the first place. It took me a long afternoon of searching to locate the Holt, when I first looked in the 1970s.

It was a hot and balmy day and I tramped up and down the hillside above the Dart for a good few hours without success. Then I dug William Crossing's *Guide to Dartmoor* out of my rucksack and scanned it for a clue. In an almost throwaway line the great Crossing points out that "an old track is carried from this (St Raphael's Chapel) to Week Ford at Wo Brook Foot. By following this the Piskies Holt may be reached".

Well, that was what I had done. So far, so good. Then I noticed the bit I had overlooked: "It is marked by four sycamores". The problem was there were lots of trees in the vicinity and a fair few sycamores.

In the end I came upon the cave quite unexpectedly, and it was much nearer to Dartmeet than I had envisaged, and a trifle further away from the river. But it was quite a cave. I knelt down to crawl inside and then found I could stand up. It was good and dry inside and curiously light. Others had already found their way here, for tucked into one wall were a fair number of silver coins and silver pins, no doubt deposited to propitiate the little fellows. It was a long cave and there was a further 'emergency escape' entrance at the far end through which I climbed up to the surface.

I dug once more into my rucksack and brought out my copy of Crossing's *Tales of the Dartmoor Pixies*. Here was a lavish description of what I had just seen and I cannot better William Crossing's description:

"It is a long narrow passage formed by large slabs of granite resting on two natural walls of the same. It is curved in form and extends for a distance of thirty-seven feet. Its width is about four feet, and it is of sufficient height for a man to stand upright in it. The entrance, which is but two-and-a-half feet in height is at the eastern end, and at the other extremity is a small aperture through which it is possible to climb out of the cave. The floor is covered with decayed leaves, blown in by the wind".

Having exited from the far end I went back to the main entrance and crawled inside once more. The leaves on the floor had shown no signs of disturbance on my first exploration, but clearly someone had been in very recently, for a brand new five pence had fallen down from the wall. In fact there were several pounds worth of silver coins and around a hundred pins lining the wall. Clearly someone had great faith in Piskies.

I dwelt for a while on the phenomenon of Dartmoor Piskies. In fact they have a number of other supposed lairs on Dartmoor, not least the famous cave on Sheepstor. Tales of their antics abound. I commend William Crossing's volumes or Ruth St Leger Gordon's *Witchcraft and Folklore of Dartmoor,* if you wish to delve further into the subject. I might as well say here that I have never personally seen a Dartmoor Pisky, though I have observed a lot of odd things on Dartmoor and had several weird experiences. Years ago, I used to know a Dartmoor vicar who often walked northern Dartmoor. He assured me in all seriousness that he had often witnessed pisky activity in the more lonesome stretches of his parish. He told me of a number of instances when he had had a close up view. Whether I believed him or not is hardly the point. *He* clearly believed in what he was saying.

In those days I used to spend a great many nights on Dartmoor, bivvying amidst whatever shelter I could find. It seemed to me that the Pixies Holt would make an admirable halfway point for long expeditions across the Moor. I tried it out a week or two later. After a hot day's walking and a dip in the Dart, I crawled inside for the night. It was a peaceful and restful experience. And I didn't see a single pisky – despite the couple of pints I had enjoyed at the Forest Inn at Hexworthy on my journey. What I do recall feeling was a wonderful sense of security, as though I had a force field wrapped around me. I used the Holt as one of my Dartmoor bedrooms on many occasions after that.

I have to confess that I haven't been to the Pixies Holt now for many years. I hope it is the same and unspoiled and that other visitors have left silver coins and pins to keep the Piskies happy. If you do visit please treat their home with respect and leave a silvery tribute. You never know – they might be watching you!

A Walk by the River Otter

One of my favourite shorter walks is the several miles of coastline between Ladram Bay and the mouth of the River Otter in east Devon, returning along the banks of the Otter to the attractive village of Otterton. Probably no more than seven miles in total, but with some glorious changes of scenery. If you are driving you can park free by Otterton village green if you get there first thing in the morning, which happens to be the best time to do this cracking ramble.

Walking up the village street, you fork left at the top – the lane leading to Sidmouth – and just past the bus turning bay a footpath heads uphill to the right. This used to be quite a wide green lane, but is now a narrower path. At the top of the first slope, it turns briefly to the left, then hard right uphill along the edge of a field. This is a good viewpoint, offering wide vistas over the east Devon heathlands, with the Iron Age hill fort of Woodbury Castle in the distance in one direction, and Mutter's Moor and Peak Hill above Sidmouth in the other. At the head of the field, the path becomes enclosed again, exiting on to a country lane. Turn left along this for just a few yards, then right on to an unsurfaced track. Head along this, past a couple of modern houses to the next road junction, with some farm cottages nearby.

Turn left here and follow the lane and then path until the South West Coastal Path is reached. Then it is just a question of turning right through a shooting gate and following the coast path until the estuary of the River Otter is reached, with the genteel resort of Budleigh Salterton on the far bank. Along the way you pass the ruins of a World War II weapons training building, an evocative reminder of Britain in the front line. Brandy Head itself tells us that this was very much a smuggling coast, used by the famous smuggler Jack Rattenbury of Beer, and Ambrose Stapleton, the smuggling vicar of nearby East Budleigh.

The coast path winds inland above the estuary of the River Otter, before coming out on to a lane, by the entrance to a farm. Keep left, crossing the river at White Bridge. There are usually fish to see in its waters, and a great deal of water fowl at the right times of the year. Just after the bridge, turn right through a gate and follow the river upstream all the way to Otterton. Not many centuries ago, the Otter was navigable all the way up to the old port of Budley Haven, below the present East Budleigh. The young Walter Raleigh, who was born not far away, probably encountered his first-going ships here.

I always find this a delightful walk and have completed it in all seasons of the year and even at night. It is best done on windless days as otherwise you will battle in exposed places against prevailing south westerly's. There is usually a lot of birds to see and there is a hide by the Otter estuary.

A Walk from Arundel

On the South Downs, England's latest National Park. An opportunity to do a favourite walk of mine from Arundel, through Arundel Park and to the delightful old church at South Stoke. This is lovely walking country.

I walked up past Swanbourne Lake, busy with August visitors, who thronged its banks and rowed across its waters, a real honeypot on such a nice day. But as always with these tourist spots, walk a few hundred yards and you leave the people behind. By the time I was in the deep valley of Arundel Park, a fold in the downland itself, I was completely alone, apart from the sheep and pheasants. These far parts of Arundel Park have to be one of the most peaceful parts of England. A gentle climb on a wide chalk track brought me up to a wooded ridge, with far distant views over the vale of the River Arun, Amberley Wild Brooks, and the high downlands above Burpham.

There is a bench I like to sit on at this point, a timeless place away from the world, where all is still and you can see for miles. If you are reading this you might like to seek it out. One of those places, a bit like a mountain summit, that is hard to leave, the restful atmosphere thereabouts a welcome relief from the speed and bustle of modern life.

Tearing myself away, I walked down to the Arun itself, beyond the great wall of Arundel Park, a veritable masterpiece of building in flint. All the way along the river I saw no one, not even in the tiny village of South Stoke, where you will find one of my favourite old parish churches in England, delightful in its simplicity, still lit only by candles, its quiet churchyard a haven of peace, where the walker might sit for ages on a bench and hear only the sounds of nature. If you cannot find peace of mind sitting in the churchyard at South Stoke, then there is something seriously wrong.

A walk along the Arun brought me back into the crowds by the Black Rabbit pub, all enjoying themselves in their own way, albeit different that day to mine. There is a lot to see around Arundel, with its castle, wildlife and wetland centre, antiquarian bookshop and antique shops, not to mention a shop devoted to the sale of new and old walking sticks. But the best thing of all is the setting, the fine River Arun circling to the south, and the folds of down and woodland around its northern boundaries.

The poet Edward Thomas wrote that the way out of Arundel to the north was a heaven on earth. I agree. And let us hope that the area's peace and tranquillity, amid the crowded counties of the south east, last for an eternity for walkers and those seeking the simple pleasures of life to enjoy. If you are seeking a break from the turmoil of this 21st century, you could do worse than walk the chalk paths of this entrancing district of the Sussex Downlands.

Winter on the Downs

On a frozen day in February I was on the South Downs, walking up to Rackham Hill from Burpham. The village stands at the end of a lane that is a terminus for motor traffic, but continues in several directions for those on foot or horseback. Burpham's church was begun in Saxon times, standing hard by the earthen banks of a hill fort. Whether that was built by Saxons or Danes is subject of much dispute. In the first half of the last century its vicar was Tickner Edwardes, who wrote some delightful books on the countryside and the craft of keeping bees. Burpham is a delightful village. John Ruskin commented that he would live there if Coniston didn't exist.

I took the lane to High Peppering, passing a herd of bison in a field as I set out. These Downs are covered in antiquities and a tumulus known as the Burgh was the first on my route. Even in February skylarks danced almost invisibly in the heights, the great sweep of downland alive with their song. The hillside was a gentle acclivity, just steep enough to make me warm up and breathe in the fresh air. The chalk was frozen hard and slippery, walking had to be done with care. I was following an ancient pathway, leading up from Burpham and the valley of the Arun to the important route that followed the ridge of the higher Downs.

I find it humbling, walking the ways people have journeyed for countless millennia. These tracks, now the recreational delight of walker and rider remain functional - farmers still use them. Sheep are driven here, as they have been since man first farmed the Downs. They grazed beside me, making an occasional sound to add to the singing of the larks. I watched them as the combatants of past wars, the pedlars, the pilgrims and other travellers of times gone must have done.

There is a timelessness about so much of our countryside, as though you could glance sideways and see history relived all around. In a sense you can for the traces of the past are everywhere. Within view of these old tracks are prehistoric flint mines, field systems and burial mounds. An hour's wandering brought me to Rackham Banks, an immense earthwork of deep trenches and mighty ramparts. Its purpose is debatable, but as I sat there in a freezing breeze I could not help but consider how much work was involved in the construction.

The slight haze from the early frost had lifted. I could see for many miles. Amberley Wild Brooks were flooded, offering an irregular silver sheen in the plain at the foot of the hill. In another direction were the downs and borstals of Arundel Park, white with ice. A herd of Friesian cattle huddled together out of the wind on the leeward slope of Amberley Mount. Tearing myself away I climbed on to the ridge path running over Rackham Hill, now part of the South Downs Way National Trail. Despite a height of just a few hundred feet it seemed as though I was on top of the world. And in a sense I was for every trace of the stress which comes with everyday living had vanished.

A Walk on Kerrera

Just a five minute ferry ride across from near Oban is the island of Kerrera. Delightful coast and moorland walking, fantastic views across to the Argyll mainland and out towards several Hebridean islands. Our walk took place on one of the hottest days I have ever known in Scotland. A perfect day for a walk.

We chose to do the southern circuit of the island, from the ferry landing, so that we might see Gylen Castle and the views towards Jura. The walk around the island is on a good track, with reasonable gradients. There are many reminders that Kerrera was once part of the kingdom of Norway. It is not difficult to imagine Viking longships slipping into the quiet coves of this island.

One of the first places you come to, walking southwards, is Horseshoe Bay, where in 1249 Alexander II of Scotland began his campaign to reclaim the Hebrides from Norwegian control. His campaign never got off the ground. He was taken ill and died in a field nearby; called Dail Righ, the king's field to this day. In 1263, a fleet of one hundred and twenty longships, under the command of Norway's King Haakon I, moored here on the way to defeat at the Battle of Largs. Kerrera is so unspoiled it feels like it all happened yesterday. At the next inlet, Little Horseshoe Bay is a row of delightful cottages, once the homes of quarry workers, before becoming the centre of the local lobster industry.

A mile further on is Gylen Castle, standing gaunt and mysterious on its clifftop above the swirling waters of the Atlantic. Okay - I admit they weren't swirling when we got there. In fact the Atlantic was still and blue. But the atmosphere of this old ruin sinks into your imagination. Gylen Castle is a place haunted by bloody deeds. It could have come straight out of a story by Scott, or Neil Munro, or John Buchan. It cries out to be in a novel. In 1647, it was besieged by Leslie's covenanters, who forced the garrison of clan MacDougall to surrender, slaughtering all the defenders, except one youth, as they came out. The castle was put to the torch, and has been abandoned ever since. We sat for a while on the stony beach nearby. All was perfect peace. It felt like the edge of the world. Souls can grow calm in places like that.

Nearby we found refreshment at a tea garden before continuing our journey. They have a bunkhouse as well, if you are tempted to spend some time on this jewel in the Firth Of Lorne.

The western side of the island became wilder as we made our way northwards, the track narrower, but with superb views towards Mull and Morvern. At Bar-nam-Boc-Bay are the remains of what was once a port, a crossing point to Mull, a place where thousands of cattle a year were brought from the islands by drovers. You can almost hear the cry of the men and the lowing of the cattle amidst its ruins.

Here we began to cross the island, back to the ferry, taking in the highest grounds of the walk. This high stretch is called Am Maolan – the Wild Place – and wild it is, seeming far higher and more remote than its contours would suggest. A long descent brought us back to Kerrera's Victorian schoolhouse, and to the four o'clock ferry, which we caught with just half a minute to spare. If you haven't been to Kerrera, then I can recommend it. The memories are priceless. A day out of the madness that we call modern life.

Walking the Connel Coach Road

The town of Oban has always been a joy to me, and some of the happiest days of my life have been spent there. If I am spared to be old, long past days of walking, I will sit quite happily by Oban's harbour watching the ferries sail out past the Isle of Kerrera to the Hebrides, and watch the sun set behind the mountains of Mull. Someone once described Oban as Scotland's Charing Cross and I can see what they mean. It is a town of bustle and determination. A staging post to distant places. You may linger there for a week or even two, but eventually you move on. Oban never leaves your memory and my heart leaps with joy every time I return. I feel something like an exile if a year passes without me walking the great curve of its bay.

But many of its visitors never explore the peaceful, rolling countryside just a mile or two inland. For all the people in the town of Oban, I doubt one in a thousand seeks out the Connel coach road. Even at the foot of Glencruitten, which starts when you are barely out of the town, it is hard to spot anyone who is not a resident, or a sportsman making their way up to the sweeping greens of the golf course. The many acres of rolling moorland, sheep country filled with good looking healthy beasts, is a place of peace, a location lost in time. By the time you head up the old lane past Acha na Lairig and out on to the coach road itself even these few people have been left behind. On a summer's day your only companions are the sheep and the skylarks.

The coach road itself, long bypassed by the modern road, is not some rough track, though it is undoubtedly on the line of some ancient route. It is even surfaced, after a fashion, and it is still just possible to take a vehicle along it. Not that I ever seen anything but a postal van, and then at the other end on its way to the farm at Achavaich. Even the railway line that runs parallel to the road doesn't seem to detract from the wildness of the walk.

Before the building of the line this must have been quite a wild approach to Oban. A good place for a deadly ambush, for you could hide an army in the bumps and hollows of the surrounding moorland. I once climbed one of the little round hills east of the railway and, lying flat on it heather summit, watched unobserved as the farmer rounded up his sheep.

It is fun on such occasions to sink back into the imaginative play of childhood and think yourself Alan Breck or Richard Hannay on the run from determined pursuers. The good thing about living in a world dominated by books and vagabondage is that you never have to grow up. Walking gives you the opportunity to get on very close terms with your imagination, a facility often lost as you age.

The views on this low-level walk are quite superb, across Ardmucknish Bay to Benderloch, the friendly little height of Beinn Lora, with Beinn Bhreac beyond and then the mightier peaks of Cruachan, tussling with a cap of cloud. Far out to sea I could see the rain clouds gathering. Maybe an hour before the steady autumn day succumbed to grey weather. Never mind, I would be in Connel by then. And soon I was, walking along the shore, looking up at the long line of small hotels and bed and breakfast establishments. On my way to visit the Black Lochs of Kilvaree....

The Black Lochs of Kilvaree

After walking the Connel Coach Road I walked the length of Connel itself, making a short diversion on to the dramatic Connel Bridge, which crosses the mouth of Loch Etive. Below are the Falls of Lora, a dramatic swirling of water tidal race where loch meets sea. Then under the railway line and on to the track, winding out on to open moorland, leading to the Black Lochs of Kilvaree.

I first discovered the Black Lochs (there are three, or rather two, for there is a connection between the two northern lochs and the southern loch is extremely reed-strewn) back in 1996, when I was staying in Benderloch and seeking an easy walk after a gruelling day on the peaks of Cruachan. I have walked by them several times since in all kinds of weather. Apart from a distant sheep farmer or two I have never seen a soul. And yet bustling Oban is only a couple of miles away. The surrounding countryside to the west of the lochs is mostly moorland and rough grazing. The opposite banks are delightfully wooded.

As you begin the climb to the lochs there are excellent views over Loch Etive, with Beinn Lora beyond. For those interested in Irish mythology, this is the exile country of Deirdre of the Sorrows and her lover. I won't repeat the tale here, but there are some fair versions online and in old books.

I halted for a break on the ruined wall of a house, a habitation or shieling perhaps, I'm not sure. On the hilltop above is a dramatic hanging boulder. I usually stop here, though I find it an eerie place, one of those bits of wild country where the boundaries of the present and past seem particularly close. Even the crows, who have followed me for the past mile, have fallen silent.

I have always had a feeling that the real Stone of Destiny is hidden hereabouts. Just a feeling, nothing more. The block now in Edinburgh, which was once in Westminster Abbey, is clearly not the original crowning seat of the kings of Scotland, which from all contemporary descriptions was something far more elaborate. Don't know why I feel it here, but I just do. I was interested, reading Andrew Greig's Stone of Destiny thriller *Romanno Bridge*, to find that he sets several scenes not far away.

Not even a dog barked as I passed the farm at Kilvaree, though one usually does. I walked past the southernmost loch, mostly reed, before climbing the hill to Ardconnel. From here a quiet country lane winds back to via the delightful Luachrach Loch, where I fed the ducks and swans, back to an Oban that was busy with people. It felt like I had wandered into its streets from another world.

Return to Glen Tilt

On a good clear April day we walked up into Glen Tilt from Blair Atholl, along the Glen Tilt track, that once disputed right of way. Patches of snow still clung to the highest mountains and the top edges of the glen. Lapwings called as they flew overhead. After Gaws Bridge, the glen becomes much more rugged and, in the vicinity of Forest Lodge, there are crags on the slopes above the river. Every now and again a few snowflakes would fall out of a seemingly blue sky and the temperature would dip.

The River Tilt was in sprawling, energetic mood, rocks smoothed over hundreds of years of its fearsome passage. Its lower stretches are half-hidden by delightful patches of woodland, a splendid stand of beech trees by the lovely Gilbert's Bridge. At Forest Lodge, a vast establishment for deer stalkers, built in 1789 and much used by the Victorian Establishment, eight miles up a rough track, you really get a feel of the isolation of the glen. It stands like some outpost in the Wild West, far from civilisation, far from anything very much to do with the 21st century. If you are very well off, or have lots of buddies to chip in, you can rent the place for a break from the Atholl Estates. If you are a seriously-loaded stravaiger I can see its charms. A good base to explore these lonely hills.

As we headed a little way further, above the lodge, a ferocious wind tore its way down the glen. Then, as we turned a corner, the glen became still and sheltered once more, the sun warming between the tiny bursts of snow.

Walking back that day, we saw a young red deer stag just a few yards away, obviously so unused to people that he had no fear, feeding regardless. Just one deer seen in so vast a deer forest. In all we walked seventeen miles in this magnificent glen. If you want a sheltered walk I commend it to you.

Walking in the Atholl Deer Forest

Into the hills above Blair Atholl hoping to hear stags bellow. The car park below Glen Tilt was chock full of ramblers from Edinburgh, as we squeezed into the last available space, setting out ahead of them up Glen Banvie, following the waters of the Banvie Burn. The autumn colours were nearly there, but needed a week or two to be at their most glorious. Passing through the deer fence at the edge of the woodland, we headed out on to the hill, first above the Banvie Burn, then up a stalkers track across the Allt na Moine Baine water and then around the slopes of Carn Dearg Beag.

Then out into wilder countryside above the waters of Allt an t-Seapail. As we approached the little wooden bridge across the tumbling burn, we heard the distant bellowing of a stag somewhere around the misty heights of Beinn Dearg. Not as loud as some I have heard before, but still unearthly, an echoing vibrational tone of raw nature. As we headed over to the edges of Glen Bruar we heard another stag bellow, the air filling with the sound, albeit still at a distance. A grouse jumped from the heather with its loud cry of "Go Back"!

One of the reasons people go hillwalking, I suppose, is to get away from the turmoil of modern life. Looking across the vast mountains and moorlands of Atholl, it seemed a world away from grubby politicians holding meaningless party conferences where the hopes and desires of most of society seem to be ignored. Putting on the news that night I thought how our politicians might benefit from days in the hills. Few do nowadays, compared to the happy decades when it was not unusual to see Cabinet Ministers out on the Pennine Way or tallying up their latest Munro.

In wildness lies the hope of the world, to paraphrase the poet. A good hard day in the hills, feeling the cold air sweep up the course of a highland burn and hearing a stag bellow might do our politicians the world of good.

Climbing The Church Tower At Ranworth

I can remember when it was often possible to climb church towers across England. These days it is a rare privilege. So it was a great treat on the recent visit to Norfolk to be able to climb the tower of St Helen's church at Ranworth – the Cathedral of the Broads. Better still, it was on a beautiful clear morning with distant views across the Broads and surrounding countryside. Patches of blue water and boats making their lazy way across Ranworth Broad and the River Bure.

First came 89 winding, tight and uneven stone steps, then a metal ladder and a wooden ladder past the bells, a push-up of a trapdoor and out on to the top of the tower, some 96 feet above the ground. As the church guide book says, "The View! Like the ascent, the panorama is breathtaking." It certainly is! I am always full of admiration for the masons that built this. My grandfather worked as a steeplejack. I envied him his work this day.

The church is well worth a visit even if you don't climb the tower. The 15th century painted medieval screen is the best example in England with clear portrayals of saints and apostles. There is a beautifully coloured Antiphoner – a real work of art and both new and old misericords. I like exploring these old churches, so much a direct link with the people of the past. Ranworth's church is one of the best, their guidebook one of the most comprehensive I have encountered. Across the churchyard is a splendid tearoom run by parish volunteers, welcome after the climb up the tower.

Chapter Seven: Trespassing Days And Ways

Some Notes for the Prospective Trespasser: In Chapter Three I gave a brief introduction to the law regarding trespass and the possible consequences for those who feel the urge to walk away from rights of way and access land. I am in no way, by the thoughts and comments in this chapter, advocating that people trespass. But it has to be noted that many of the rights we all enjoy today - not least our right to walk in the countryside at all - are only there because people stretched the letter of the law by acts of civil disobedience. We would probably never have had the CRoW Act, the Scottish Land Reform legislation, or even many of our footpaths and bridleways but for those pioneer ramblers who pushed the boundaries.

I have to confess to being an inveterate trespasser. If you feel the urge to follow in my footsteps, then on your own head be it! Many of our parents and grandparents fought for this country in various wars. Why is it deemed okay to be prepared to die for your country, but not be allowed to walk across it? Why should the returning war hero be deemed a trespasser for wanting to enjoy the best of our countryside?

In his remarkable essay *In Praise of Walking*, Sir Leslie Stephen, writer, philosopher, first editor of the *Dictionary of National Biography*, and the father of the novelist Virginia Woolf, made no bones about his enthusiasm for trespass when out on his long country walks:

When once beyond the "town," I looked for notices that trespassers would be prosecuted that gave a strong presumption that the trespass must have some attraction. To me it was a reminder of the many delicious bits of walking which, even in the neighbourhood of London, await the man who has no superstitious reverence for legal rights. It is indeed surprising how many charming walks can be contrived by a judicious combination of a little trespassing with the rights of way happily preserved over so many commons and footpaths.

Like Sir Leslie Stephen I have no superstitious reverence for legal rights of property. Why shouldn't the British people walk as freely as possible around their own countryside? I always have. That doesn't mean I walk everywhere. I don't walk through growing crops unless they are obstructing a public right of way, I have no interest in accessing people's gardens or the immediate policies of people's houses. But it seems to me that wider areas of the countryside, barred to the British people for no good reason, are fair game.

Recent access legislation has given us access to mountain and moorland, heath and downland, and common land. But that has opened up only a small percentage of the British landscape. We are still denied access to much of our native woodland, river banks and coastline, low-lying pastures and meadows, and the parklands of many of our great estates.

You must, of course, trespass with care. Nobody ever knows that the successful trespasser has ever been in the vicinity. Cause no damage. Leave no litter. Be careful when crossing gates, hedges and fences. But exercise your right to roam. Given those provisos, there is no reason on earth why England and Wales cannot enjoy the freedom to roam over so much more of our land. That is why I shall continue to campaign for access legislation at least equivalent to that in Scotland and much of the rest of Europe. Please do read the comments on trespass in chapter three and the Blue Book on rights of way law. *It is the choice of every walker whether he or she decides to trespass, but please do be aware of the consequences. On your own head be it!*

Land Access and Trespassing: It always amazes me that a minority of people who own vast tracts of land resent sharing their acres with everyone else. Surely land is the common heritage of us all? Nobody made it, though generations have used it. In Scotland, before the *Land Reform Act*, there was a long tradition of free access, though that didn't stop some landowners trying to keep people out. A few individuals are still resisting the Act. England and Wales are poorly served. While the CRoW (*Countryside and Rights of Way Act*) supposedly gives access to mountain, moorland, heath, downs and common land, there are still huge areas where landowners have argued that those categories don't apply. Despite its good intentions, CRoW doesn't give you free access to much of England's downland or places like Vixen Tor and over twenty other heights in the Dartmoor National Park.

How long will English and Welsh ramblers have to wait before we have access legislation on the Scottish model? How long before we can access the coastline of England? How long before we can walk freely in our forests and woodlands? Time to get some hard-hitting campaigns under way!

Battles between landowners and the people are nothing new of course. Attempts to close old tracks and even wider stretches of land have led to a number of battles in and out of the legal system. The Commons, Open Spaces and Footpaths Preservation Association (to give it its formal present-day name, though better known as The Open Spaces Society) was founded in 1865 and was an early participant in the resistance against countryside denial – as it does now as the oldest of our national conservation and access groups. A number of other footpath preservation groups were established during the nineteenth century, particularly in the vicinity of the

Britain's fast-growing towns and cities; in York as early as 1824 and Manchester in 1826.

Nor were these necessarily rebellious working class organisations. Archibald Prentice, in his fascinating book on the history of Manchester, describes the members of the Manchester Association for the Preservation of Ancient Footpaths as a mixture of 'Tories, Whigs and Radicals' who "spread among the country gentlemen a wholesome terror of transgressing against the right of the poor to enjoy their own without anyone to make them afraid."

Many of the working class labourers who wished to avail themselves of the neighbouring countryside had that love of nature mentioned by Elizabeth Gaskell in her novel *Mary Barton*. With increased education and political empowerment, members of the working class began to look beyond the working week to their brief hours of leisure, the moorlands so close to the places of work being a great temptation and escape. James Bryce described the frustrations of these restrictions in 1892:

If, for instance, I was going to the top of a mountain, and saw in the distance the cliffs overhanging a loch, I am not to be prevented from going to that loch because it happens to be in a deer forest and off the footpath. That destroys all the sense of joyous freedom which constitutes the great part of the enjoyment of fine scenery.

These comments were made in a speech in the House of Commons, Bryce being not only a Member of Parliament but, at other times in his career, Professor of Civil Law at Oxford University, a member of the Cabinet in the Liberal Government, and Britain's Ambassador to the United States. He was to have a political career that was rich in rewards, including the Order of Merit and a peerage. But words were not enough for Bryce. From 1884 onwards he and his brother Annan tabled several Bills that might give a legal right of access to mountains. They were all to fail, despite having considerable cross-party support.

When Annan Bryce's Access to Mountains Bill was debated in the Commons in 1908, he received considerable support from the Tory Opposition and the blessing of the Liberal Government. A fervent supporter was a young MP named Winston Churchill (who attended land reform rallies where he called for land nationalisation, and led the crowds in the song *God Made the Land for the People*), and Ramsey MacDonald for the Labour Party, who told the House that he had often trespassed in Scottish deer forests. Sadly, the Bill was lost through lack of time. Trespassing continued and the war on the ground became increasingly bitter.

In the aftermath of the Great War there was a strong feeling that the British people – many of whom had endured the horror of the trenches – should be able to roam around the country they had fought for. The philosopher C.E.M. Joad made no bones about it when he wrote in one of his many books "I should regard it as a form of shirking, if I refrained from trespassing when private property lay in my path." Such incitement to walk across forbidden Britain was not so unusual at the time. The journalist Stephen Graham could see little harm in trespassing adventures, remarking that 'it is neither so wicked nor so dangerous to be a trespasser as might at first appear.'

That was not necessarily the case. In some parts of Britain trespassers could become the victims of overt acts of violence and conflict and danger was not unusual. But as more people headed out into the countryside in the decades between the World Wars, there were fresh battles and memorable battlegrounds, for rambling was no longer just the pursuit of the middle classes, the intellectuals and the literary.

From the end of Queen Victoria's reign rambling clubs for working and lower middle class walkers were becoming commonplace and walkers were regularly heading into disputed territory. These battles came to a head in the 1930s when the grouse moors of the Peak District and Yorkshire became the cockpit of the battles for access. It is worth remembering that ramblers only gained access to many of these moorlands with the implementation of the CRoW (*Countryside and Rights of Way Act*) a decade ago. The English, Welsh and Irish peoples are still denied access to some of the best areas of landscape in the British Isles.

In the 1930s, C.E.M. Joad pointed out that in the 230 square miles of moorland between Manchester and Sheffield there were only twelve public rights of way of more than two miles long and that "of the 150,000 acres involved; only 1,212 acres are open to the public." Nor were private owners the only transgressors. Joad criticised the local authorities who denied ratepayers access to 39,000 acres of moorland.

A Sheffield rambler of the time, Phil Barnes, complained that "although Bleaklow is only sixteen miles in a straight line from the centres of Manchester and Sheffield, there are, surrounding this ridge, thirty-seven square miles of wild country, quite unknown except to a few ramblers who defy the unjust restrictions and take the access so far denied them by law." Barnes mapped and photographed these forbidden lands, publishing at his own expense a book which became a starting point for those claiming that there should be increased public access. The idea of just being confined to paths was abhorrent to Barnes:

No true hill lover wants to see more footpaths in the wild heart of the Peak each nicely labelled with trim signposts and bordered by notices telling one not to stray. What he does want is the simple right to wander where fancy moves him – to seek the highest ridges, to scramble along the rocky sides of cloughs. In a wilderness of this sort a public footpath to which one is expected to stay is a restriction which offends, although the moor may not be fenced off with a physical barrier.

He was not alone in his quest. Mainstream rambling books published in the 1930s positively incited walkers to trespass, often giving full accounts of the wonderful territory that might be explored by the bold and adventurous. The popular walker and writer A.J. Brown wandered freely across the pre-War moorlands of Yorkshire and featured his rambles in a succession of delightful books:

*I will confess (*he wrote*) that I am one of those rebels who believe that the moors and waste-lands are common-lands – much too vast and good for any one person to keep exclusively to himself – path or no path. Trespassers "will be prosecuted" (Perhaps). – All Yorkshiremen are "trespassers" (of sorts) at heart, and it will be a bad day for the country when they lose their native independence and instinctive resistance to any sort of encroachment on their natural rights.*

If trespassing is for you then do try my other book "The Compleat Trespasser."

A Woodland Trespass:

In the south of England is a forest of over three hundred acres, surrounded on three sides by the curve of a river, the fourth side edged by a busy main road. This oakwood was once a Chase, a hunting ground from Norman times and part of one of the great manorial estates of the county. In times past the harsh laws that applied to many such hunting grounds, with mutilation, fines and imprisonment applied to anyone caught transgressing these manor grounds. In Regency and Victorian times, the chase was strictly preserved for shooting, no doubt with man traps and spring guns set to deter interlopers. Yet even then there was recognition of the woodland's beauty. In the nineteenth-century an enlightened landowner built carriage drives that contoured the hillsides, so that his friends and visitors might better see the exquisite views over the swirling waters of the river.

One guidebook author, writing in the years before the Great War, tells us that the then landowner opened up the carriage drives to the public on certain days of the week, showing at least some commitment to sharing such beauty with others. It is a dramatic landscape, the wooded hillside falling steeply from an Iron Age hill fort to the white waters of a mighty river; great rocky tors rising steeply both from the hillside and the river banks. There was once some industry here, for hidden deep in the undergrowth are the shafts and adits of ancient mine workings.

While the Chase is no longer preserved for game, some local people have a concession for occasional rough shooting, and a fisherman or two might be seen near to the little footbridge on summer evenings. For such a vast area there is a limited amount of wildlife as much of it was cleared in earlier days. The empty badger setts speak volumes about the past ferocity of unenlightened gamekeepers towards Britain's native wildlife. The near-island status of the woodland has made natural re-colonization difficult, though some mammals have been put back over the past few years.

There is no absolute refusal of entry to the forest and river banks. The landowner is not opposed to limited access by written permission. But the general public is discouraged. There are few access points. High wire fences and locked gates greet the visitor in the area adjacent to the nearest public car park. The fast-flowing river is sufficient deterrent to all but the brave or foolhardy.

I had not walked through the woodlands of the Chase for some years, until my trespass. I had had no plans to go there on that quiet Tuesday but, seeing the autumnal woods from the opposite hillside proved too great a temptation. I had had a fraught meeting earlier in the day and felt the need to unwind in some wild place. There were not many cars on the road, so I climbed over the hedge bank and plunged into the cover of the wood. There were one or two nearby houses, but no one was about as I headed along the brow of the hill along one of the now overgrown Victorian carriage drives. This rutted trail bore little sign that anyone had been there recently; there were the hoof prints of horses and old boot marks, but no suggestion of fresher human tracks in its muddy ruts.

You get a strange feeling walking through great woodlands knowing that although this is urbanised southern England, there is no one close at hand. A fall here could mean that you might not be found for days or even weeks. Although this should be a perilous sensation it is not. It is comforting that there are such places where we can still be totally in thrall to nature in all its wildness, a far cry from the over-comfortable state in which most of us exist if not actually live.

For the trespasser there is then the contrary feeling that perhaps you are *not* alone. You search the trees and the undergrowth for the watching eyes and even though you sink into a mood of pure relaxation, though your nerves are geared up to the possibility of ambush. You think of what you might say if you are challenged. Will you be aggressive or submissive? Will there be a moment of violence or just mutual embarrassment? You look for side paths so that you might slink away if you hear other footsteps, the crack of a dry twig, or someone's conversation. The true trespasser seeks avoidance and not confrontation, unless it be an occasion when you really want to make a political point.

Walking beneath the highest trees in the chase is like progressing through the arches of some great cathedral. There is stateliness about such trees, inducing a feeling of awe that there should be such wondrous creations on the face of the Earth. Even in a Devon autumn there is a great deal of cover left, magnificent leaves of every shade of brown and russet, continually adding in the gentle breeze to the thick carpet of vegetation at your feet. Even the wider tracks are hidden by lost leaves and sometimes obstructed by branches brought down in the year's gales.

As I strolled on I came to a vast open space surrounded on all sides by the forest, the track I was following forcing a way alongside a tiny stream. There were roe deer grazing not far from the woodland edge some feeding and others standing sentinel, regarding each area of the woodland boundary for threatening intruders. I was walking with the prevailing wind at my back, but the depth of the trees and undergrowth dispersed the air currents in all directions and gave no hint of my approach. I lay down alongside the roots of an oak and watched the deer for nearly an hour – a real privilege to see them in such a natural setting. I have watched deer in these woods before, not just the roe but red deer that have made the long journey from Exmoor, and the strange little muntjac with their noisy bark, introduced to the area by some past landowner.

I wondered how to progress on my journey without disturbing the deer when the matter was taken out of my hands. First one, then another, then all the deer looked up. I knew why. A harsh crack of a snapped tree bough echoed up from the valley, followed by the crash of someone forcing their way uphill through the scrub. The outer branches of a holly shivered and a man emerged on to the track. The deer had not waited for his appearance, but had disappeared into the forest on the opposite side of the clearing. I knew the man. He was an estate worker who had the occasional duty of patrolling the chase in search of interlopers. He was quite elderly, with a ruddy face and grey hair straddling out from beneath an old tweed cap. He paused on the track out of breath from the arduous climb up from the river and the fishermen's footbridge.

I considered at first that I might have been seen entering the chase and the man sent over to find me, but decided that it was pure coincidence that we were together in the woodland. He didn't seem to be searching for anyone, just enjoying a work day on his own and away from managerial eyes. I slid away from the oak and backwards into deeper vegetation, keeping him in sight all the while. Just as well as a moment later he turned down the track towards me. I watched as he passed within a few feet, obviously unaware of my presence, breathing heavily as he negotiated the fallen branches.

I sometimes wonder when, on a trespassing walk, whether I am passing hidden watchers in exactly that same way. Woods are deep and secret places and your imagination hints that there might be a thousand hidden eyes. In olden times when the Chase was a game preserve both keeper and poacher would have been wary of being observed, watching the signs of nature for hints that they were not alone. In well preserved woods it is very difficult to move quietly at all. On a recent ramble in Sussex I must have put up a hundred very noisy pheasants in the course of a couple of miles. There is the running of the deer, the sudden bolt of rabbit and hare, even an alarmed blackbird. All give warnings that there is someone about. In farm fields cows often come to investigate the passing rambler and sheep head away from the hillwalkers on moorland and mountain. All draw the eyes and ears of those who would oppose the trespasser.

I could hear the man for nearly half an hour as he continued on his way. But I saw no more deer as I came out on to the track and set off in the opposite direction, downhill now towards the river. The path was steeper and overgrown. It was hard to imagine the Victorian trippers negotiating it by horse and carriage. They must have had exciting expeditions. How often was their sightseeing observed by some unauthorised spectator?

I heard the river long before it came into view. For a while the track contoured just above its banks for a long stretch before making one final dip towards the lower carriage drive that followed its course. It had rained heavily in the previous weeks and the high moorland was issuing forth its stored moisture. White water broke over fierce rapids. Dark and jagged rocks emerging from the thundering flow seemed to tear apart the river itself. If anything else was making a noise in that landscape it could not be heard against the roar of the river. A thousand watchers might yell disapproval at my presence but they were as silence itself against the sounds that boiled through the valley. A long length of almost pure white water led to a sudden curve in the river, where it fell into a deep and dark pool. On the opposite bank a great cliff arose from the pool, rising high above the banks and the surrounding trees.

Even in autumn little sunlight penetrated to the black waters of this quieter stretch of river. The pool is famously deep but has a forbidding atmosphere that seems to deter the swimmer. It is a place just made for suicide. Its sinister waters seem to urge you to the very act of jumping. I once intended to spend an evening there watching for otters, but felt so depressed after just an hour that I hurried away. I stayed there on my trespass for only the briefest of moments before continuing back upstream.

The carriage drive brought me to the miniature suspension bridge used by fishermen and, as the gate was unlocked, I crossed and left the privacy of the Chase behind. I had walked through one of the most magnificent landscapes in southern England, seen once again spectacular and beautiful river scenery and tramped beneath tall and majestic trees. But how sad that this land, countryside that should be the common heritage of us all, is barred to those who might most delight in its wonders.

Walking a Lost Path

Walking along an ancient ridge path I went astray and found myself trespassing. The adventure was an eye-opener – a gorgeous tramp across delightful countryside. The day had started when I wanted to pioneer a new route along which to lead a local rambling group. I set out from a village hidden deep in a green and wooded valley to the ringing of the bells from a church that dates back to Saxon times.

A steep climb up a public footpath brought me to the edge of a long hill, an ascent as hard as any you might find, which left me breathless by the time I reached its woody summit. It was a glorious spring morning with clear views across a broad agricultural vale to an Iron Age hill fort a good mile away. Coming up through the wood I had found a number of earth banks hidden amongst the trees, abandoned land boundaries that probably date to medieval times, perhaps even to the centuries when Saxon farmers worked this landscape. The hill fort itself an expression of a desire to control the land, to stamp the authority of a man's ownership on the face of the earth, and to warn passers-by that their presence was only tolerated.

But the path that travels the length of the long ridge was testament to the fact that people journeyed this way from the earliest of times. This ridgeway is probably contemporary with the hill fort, maybe even older. Walkers have journeyed atop the hill for thousands of years. Tinkers and merchants have plied their trade at the farms and hamlets along its way. Gypsies have used its hidden route to seek out camp sites where they might not be disturbed, soldiers have marched, and pilgrims talked of spiritual and temporal matters as they made their journey to other and longer pilgrim routes.

Once past the wood and a stretch of open heathland, the ridge way progresses along the highest portion of the hill, passing between the high hedgerows of farm fields. Soon after a farm the ridge way became a metalled lane, but still clearly following its traditional route. Between the gateways there were wide views over the surrounding countryside. As I emerged on to the valley's lane I wandered for a while alongside a tiny stream that gives a seaside town its name, before heading uphill, on to the opposite ridge.

This was a remarkable area, even for this amateur antiquary. A glance over the field gates showed a number of grassy mounds, the burial barrows of the Bronze Age farmers who once lived on and worked this land. They must have held the hill to be sacred, for judging by the dozens of barrows this was a burial ground without equal in this part of England. A great open space now fenced in, but which was once free heathland where the dead were buried and to which, even in recent times, there must have been open access.

A quiet lane ran right across the down, obviously the line of another ridgeway. A few hundred yards led to an ancient crossing, where it was bisected by a present-day bridleway, overgrown with gorse and bracken, but passable. It widened as I walked, clinging to the edge of the down above a deep and wooded valley. Sheep grazed the open ground to my right, strolling away as I came near to them, and moving away faster as I disturbed the pheasants that clustered in the surrounding undergrowth. Bird song filled the air, though I saw few thanks to the thickness of the leaves on the nearby trees.

Just before the ridge way crossed a lane, I passed a smallholding, something between a farm and a Gypsy encampment, with goats pressed against the fence of a tiny field that had been won from the greater space of the downland. Double gates led across the lane and on to a wider section of track. There were pheasants now in profusion, suggesting that I had entered the preserves of a shooting estate, though the bridleway was clearly waymarked and obviously well used. Woodland of oak and beech lined the valley eastwards and alongside the track were several deep goyles, natural cuttings into the chalky ground, widened by the men of the past who must have sought stone and flints from their precipitous slopes.

It was a wonderful section of ancient ridge way and it was not hard to imagine the travellers of old as they journeyed on foot or horseback. There was little gradient to my route, a barely perceptible descent scarcely noticed, whatever direction you were heading in. There were occasional glimpses of the sea, suggesting that the path may have had its origins in prehistoric times in expeditions to find salt for the preservation of meat. As I wandered downhill the track followed a slight curve of the hill, a path going off to the right. This section was more wooded and I noticed a number of pheasant pens amid the little glades. I paused often to look back the way I had come, such was the beauty of the path and the glory of the trees along the way.

It did not occur to me that I was no longer following the bridleway. Only a change in the position of the sun and the distant coastline suggested that I was heading in the wrong direction. I dug into my knapsack and pulled out the map. There it was, the line of the ridge way very clearly marked. I found the smallholding farm and the lane beyond. Then the truth dawned. The bridleway did *not* follow the ridge way beyond the curve where the tiny path had led off to the right. At some point in history the right of way had been removed from this most ancient route of passage. I looked at the alternative path on the map. It seemed purely functional, running along the edge of a field and out on to a road. Functional and artificial. A convenience more for the landowner than the walker.

Yet here I was in the midst of a beautiful countryside and obviously on what had been the ridge path of old. Why had the right of way been stolen from the people? I determined to find out. The woods were thicker now and the pheasants numerous. A number of pleasing rides led down through the trees, but there were other paths as well. Narrower routes across the valley to the east. And on one of these I found the stump of what might once have been a fingerpost, one of those delightful signs that mark the course of a public footpath.

So in past times there had been other rights of way round this estate. People had once enjoyed the freedom to roam over other paths beyond the ridge way. And not that long ago judging by the evidence of the old footpath sign. Perhaps even since the local map of all rights of way had been compiled in the 1950s. I took out the Ordnance Survey sheet and searched in vain for the slightest evidence that any rights of way existed now. But the truth dawned clear. At some time a ridge way and all of its ancillary paths, tracks that people had walked for thousands of years, had been barred to the public.

I soon found out why. The next curve of the track opened up a wider vista across the valley. There was a Georgian manor house, surrounded by a formal garden. As I looked across to the wooded coverts on the opposite side of the valley it became obvious that one landowner had created a little world of exclusion for his own benefit. It was certainly an idyllic spot, though I suspected that sporting rights were the real reason that access to the ridge way was denied. The pens and feeders suggested that the pheasant breeding was on a commercial scale. This was not one man's retreat. It was a rural business to an industrial degree.

Yet the pheasants scampered around my feet almost oblivious to my presence. These birds are not much bothered by walkers, or easily disturbed at all. It is hard enough for the beaters on a shoot to get pheasants to take to the air. The bird's preference is always to scuttle into the nearest bit of undergrowth.

I opined that a great party of walkers would have no effect on any shoot, particularly as they would be on defined paths as they made their way through the coverts. No landowner or keeper can seriously deny this. And it is no good them suggesting that public access might lead to theft or poaching. I have known a few thieves and poachers in my time and none were bothered about whether or not they were following rights of way. No one challenged me as I walked down the ridge way. I could easily have made off with a dozen pheasants.

The ridge way ended on the concreted drive to the house. I followed this up to a public highway. I was some distance from where I wanted to be, but a glance at the map showed that I could get there by a couple of miles of lane walking. It was pleasant too, offering good views across the countryside and down into the private grounds of the manor. After a mile I came across a hill fort from the Iron Age. Wooded now, its banks and ditches still covered by the last autumn's leaves. There was public access here and several people could be seen picnicking or just wandering around.

But to me these vast earthworks survive in curious isolation, for today's visitors can no longer walk freely along the prehistoric ways that came into existence to serve as its access routes. Paths which were old before the hill fort was built as prehistoric man journeyed to the Bronze Age burial sites on the Down or to the salt ways leading to the sea.

ENVOI:

Let us be always out of doors among trees and grass, and rain and wind and sun. There the breeze comes and strikes the cheek and sets it aglow; the gale increases and the trees creak and roar, but it is only a ruder music. A calm follows, the sun shines in the sky, and it is the time to sit under an oak, leaning against the bark, while the birds sing and the air is soft and sweet. By night the stars shine, and there is no fathoming the dark spaces between those brilliant points, nor the thoughts that come as it were between the fixed stars and landmarks of the mind.

Or it is the morning on the hills, when hope is as wide as the world; or it is the evening on the shore. A red sun sinks, and the foam-tipped waves are crested with crimson; the booming surge breaks, and the spray flies afar, sprinkling the face watching under the pale cliffs. Let us get out of these indoor narrow modern days, whose twelve hours somehow have become shortened, into the sunlight and the pure wind. A something that the ancients called divine can be found and felt there still.

Richard Jefferies in *The Amateur Poacher*.

Recommended Reading

Britain's countryside, rambling and access issues have been the inspiration for quite a number of Britain's writers. On this page I have listed a number of books that I have enjoyed and which you might enjoy as well. These first recommendations suggest some classic works on Forbidden Britain and the Right to Roam issue, together with my thoughts on each. Many of these books are, sadly, out of print, but most can be obtained through your local library, or through website book dealers such as Abebooks or Amazon. Anyway, here are a few recommendations:

Freedom to Roam by Howard Hill, Moorland Publishing, Derbyshire 1980. Despite the fact that Howard Hill's book has been overtaken by events, it is still the best historical introduction to the struggle for access to our countryside. Highly recommended.

The 1932 Kinder Scout Trespass by Benny Rothman, Willow Publishing, Timperley 1982. Benny Rothman was one of the leaders of the 1932 mass trespass on to Kinder Scout, which forged the way for the eventual National Parks Act and Countryside and Rights of Way Act. This is Benny's own account of that glorious day, his subsequent trial before a loaded jury, and his spell of imprisonment - gaoled for walking across his own countryside. Don't miss reading it. *Now in a splendid new edition as well. Well worth getting as well as the original, a superb read – a goodly reminder of where we have come from on land access and where we should be going. Order a copy today!* "The Battle for Kinder Scout" by Benny Rothman. Introduction by Mike Harding. Willow Publishing (Althrincham, Cheshire. ISBN 978-0-946361-44-1)

Forbidden Land by Tom Stephenson, Manchester University Press 1989. Good on most aspects of the history of the struggle for access to the countryside, but suspect in its judgement on mass trespassing.

Freedom to Roam by Harold Sculthorpe, Freedom Press, London 1993. This slim booklet takes an anarchical view of the access struggle, in a series of entertaining essays. A good follow-up to the other texts.

A Right to Roam by Marion Shoard, London 1999. Now out of date, but worth looking at for the history of how the British people were denied access to their countryside.

The Return of John Macnab by Andrew Greig, Headline London 1996. An entertaining novel that deals with some aspects of the access struggle in Scotland in the days prior to their splendid access legislation.

The Gentle Art of Walking by Geoffrey Murray, Blackie 1939. A very readable look at some of history's most famous walkers. Tells us where we are all coming from.

Shanks Pony by Morris Marples, Dent 1959. A look at literary walkers. Wonderfully readable and informative - one of my favourite books.

Scholar Gipsies by John Buchan, Many editions. A delightful and inspiring book of essays and short stories on the vagabond life. John Buchan, as well as being a noted novelist, diplomat, and historian, was a devoted walker.

The Campers and Trampers Weekend Book by Showell Styles, Seeley Service c1958. A most inspiring book on the vagabond life.

Wild Country by Sylvia Sayer, Dartmoor Preservation Association c2001. This short text looks at why we need to preserve wild countryside and our National Parks. Well worth seeking out. Lady Sayer was a true visionary.

Journey Through Britain by John Hillaby, 1968. This grand account of John Hillaby's 1960s walk from Lands End to John O'Groats, through some of the loveliest countryside in Britain, is truly inspiring and a terrific read. Makes you want to get out there and do a long trek.

Guides to the Lakeland Fells by A. Wainwright. These beautifully drawn set of guides, first published over half a century ago, have lost none of their magic. Still the best introduction to the mountains of the Lake District.

A Guide to Dartmoor by William Crossing. First published in 1909, but still the most comprehensive guide to Dartmoor. The one to read and work with before you look at any other. The best edition is the 1960s reprint with the introduction by Brian Le Messurier.

Lavengro, The Romany Rye, Wild Wales, Romano Lavo-Lil by George Borrow, Many editions. These four books give wonderful accounts of walking and the vagabond life in the 19th century.

A Shepherd's Life by W.H.Hudson, Many editions. This beautiful account of the lives of rural folk on the Wiltshire Downs is well worth reading. It gives some account of how the people were banished from the countryside, and there is a great deal of country lore.

Guerrilla Warfare by "Yank" Levy, Penguin 1941, but recent reprint. Written originally for the Home Guard, but there is a lot of useful information in this if you want to do a bit of surreptitious trespassing.

Climber's Testament by W. Kenneth Richmond, Alvin Redman 1950. A wonderful book on the philosophy of climbing mountains.

The Making of the English Landscape by W. G. Hoskins. Professor Hoskins' book is the classic work on how the land became the way it is.

The Pilgrims' Way by John Adair. A very readable introduction to some of the old pilgrim routes.

Wayfaring Life in the Middle Ages by J.J. Jusserand. A very good account of how people travelled around England in the late medieval period. Many editions.

The Old Ways by Robert MacFarlane. An atmospheric account of our ancient tracks and paths.

Navigation: Techniques and Skills for Walkers (Cicerone Mini-guide): Using Your Map and Compass by Pete Hawkins. A superb introduction to all aspects of outdoor navigation by a master navigator.

Hill Walking: The Official Handbook of the Mountain Leader and Walking Group Leader Schemes by Steve Long. A very good introduction to hillwalking and rambling in wilder places.

I hope you have enjoyed this book and found something useful within it. If you have I would be grateful if you would leave a review on this book's page on Amazon and tell your friends. I welcome suggestions and criticisms from readers which can be sent by email to stravaigerjohn.wordpress.com

Read John Bainbridge's two other books on the outdoors and walking:

The Compleat Trespasser

Footloose with George Borrow

And remember – always fight for the Right to Roam…

Printed in Great Britain
by Amazon.co.uk, Ltd.,
Marston Gate.